KU-603-972

How this publication is organised

This publication sets out the requirements for the auditing and certification of food manufacturers in order for them to achieve certification for the *Global Standard for Food Safety*.

The document consists of the following sections:

Section I Introduction
Provides an introduction and background to the development and benefits of the Standard.

Section II Requirements
Details the requirements of the Standard with which a company must comply in order to gain certification.

Section III Audit Protocol
Provides information on the audit process and rules for the awarding of certificates. This provides details of the different certification programmes available within the Standard as well as information on logos and the BRC Directory.

Section IV Operation and Governance of the Scheme
Describes the management and governance systems in place for the Standard and for the management of Certification Bodies registered to operate the scheme.

Appendices
Appendices 1 to 9 provide other useful information including auditor competency requirements, product categories and a glossary of terms.

Contents

SECTION I

INTRODUCTION

Section I

Introduction

1.1   Background

Welcome to the sixth issue of the *Global Standard for Food Safety*. Originally developed and published in 1998, the Standard has been updated at regular intervals since to reflect the latest thinking in food safety, and has now attained usage worldwide. The Standard provides a framework for food manufacturers to assist the production of safe food and to manage product quality to meet customers' requirements. Certification against the Standard is recognised by many retailers, food service companies and manufacturers around the world when assessing the capabilities of their suppliers. In response to demand, the *Global Standard for Food Safety* has been translated into many languages to facilitate implementation by food businesses across the world.

The *Global Standard for Food Safety* has been developed to specify the safety, quality and operational criteria required to be in place within a food manufacturing organisation to fulfil obligations with regard to legal compliance and protection of the consumer. The format and content of the Standard is designed to allow an assessment of a company's premises, operational systems and procedures by a competent third party – the Certification Body – against the requirements of the Standard.

1.2   What's new for Issue 6?

The sixth issue of the Standard has been developed with advice and input from working groups of international stakeholders representing food manufacturers, retailers, food service companies and Certification Bodies, and has taken into account the comments made both on Issue 5 and from the widespread consultation process.

The focus of attention for this issue has been on:

- improving consistency of the audit process

- ensuring that new developments in food safety have been effectively addressed

- providing more choice in audit options to allow sites to differentiate themselves

- encouraging adoption of the Standard as a means of improving food safety in facilities where processes are in development.

The requirements of the Issue 6 Standard are an evolution from previous issues with a continued emphasis on management commitment, an HACCP-based food safety programme and supporting quality management system. In this issue some clauses have been merged, with others expanded, most noticeably supplier management, foreign body control and allergen management. The objective has been to direct the focus of the audit towards the implementation of good manufacturing practices within the production areas. Colour coding of requirements has been introduced to highlight clauses which would normally be expected to be audited in the factory.

Voluntary unannounced programmes

There has been an increasing growth in unannounced audits amongst specifiers and this has been seen to provide a greater confidence in the implementation of a food safety culture by their suppliers. For this issue of the Standard the BRC unannounced audit programme has been developed with two options to provide choice and facilitate practical solutions to unannounced audits. The unannounced programmes remain voluntary but provide added confidence in certification to customers and creates marketing benefits where achieving the top BRC grade A+.

Enrolment programme

Whilst the unannounced audit programme may be of benefit to companies with mature food safety systems, the new BRC enrolment programme has been introduced to encourage the development of best food safety practice in factories where food safety is still developing. This scheme, which starts with registration to the BRC Directory, allows the recognition of improvements in food safety by providing a scored audit for sites that are not ready for certification. The audit reports and scores can be shared with customers and is intended to enable sites to develop within a framework that will eventually enable full certification.

Details of the new programmes can be found in the protocol of the Standard; refer to Section III.

1.3　The scope of the *Global Standard for Food Safety*

The *Global Standard for Food Safety* sets out the requirements for the manufacture of processed foods and the preparation of primary products supplied as retailer branded products, branded food products and food or ingredients for use by food service companies, catering companies and food manufacturers. Certification will only apply to products that have been manufactured or prepared at the site where the audit has taken place and will include storage facilities that are under the direct control of the production-site management.

The Standard shall not apply to food products which do not undergo any process at the site audited or to activities relating to wholesale, importation, distribution or storage outside the direct control of the company. The BRC has developed a range of Global Standards setting out the requirements for the wide range of activities undertaken in the production, packaging, storage and distribution of food. Appendix 1 provides further detail of the scopes of, and relationship between, the current Global Standards.

1.4　Food safety legislation

The Standard has always been intended to assist sites and their customers to comply with legislative requirements for food safety. Legislation covering food safety differs in detail worldwide but generally requires food businesses to:

- ensure the presence of a detailed specification which is lawful and consistent with compositional and safety standards and good manufacturing practice
- ensure they satisfy themselves that their suppliers are competent to produce the specified product, comply with legal requirements and operate appropriate systems of process control
- make visits, from time to time and where practical, to verify the competence of their suppliers or receive the result of any other audit of the supplier's system for that purpose
- establish and maintain a risk-assessed programme for product examination, testing or analysis
- monitor and act upon customer complaints.

The *Global Standard for Food Safety* has been developed to assist businesses to meet these requirements.

1.5　Benefits of the *Global Standard for Food Safety*

Adoption of the Standard leads to a number of benefits to food businesses. The Standard:

- is internationally recognised and provides a report and certification that can be accepted by customers in place of their own audits, thus reducing time and cost.
- provides a single standard and protocol that governs an accredited audit by third party Certification Bodies, allowing a credible independent assessment of a company's food safety and quality systems.
- enables certificated companies to appear on the BRC public directory, allowing recognition of their achievements and use of a logo for marketing purposes.
- is comprehensive in scope, covering areas of quality, hygiene and product safety.
- addresses part of the legislative requirements of the food manufacturer and their customers. Companies may also use this Standard to ensure their suppliers are following good food safety management practices.
- provides a range of audit options, including announced and unannounced audit programmes, to satisfy customer demands and enable companies to demonstrate compliance through a process which best suits their operation and the maturity of their food safety systems.

■   requires on-going surveillance and confirmation of the follow-up of corrective actions on non-conformity to the Standard, thus ensuring that a self-improving quality and product safety system is established.

1.6   The certification process

The *Global Standard for Food Safety* is a process and product certification scheme. In this scheme, food businesses are certificated upon completion of a satisfactory audit by an auditor employed by an independent third party – the Certification Body. The Certification Body in turn shall have been assessed and judged as competent by a national accreditation body.

In order for a food business to receive a valid certificate on completion of a satisfactory audit, the organisation must select a Certification Body approved by the BRC. The BRC lays down detailed requirements that a Certification Body must satisfy in order to gain approval.

1.7   Effective date of Issue 6

As with all revisions of the Global Standards, there must be recognition that a transition period is in place between publication and full implementation. This allows a period for the retraining of all auditors and to allow manufacturers to prepare for the new issue of the Standard. Therefore, certification against Issue 6 will commence from 1 January 2012. All certificates issued against audits carried out prior to 1 January 2012 will be against Issue 5 and be valid for the period specified on the certificate.

1.8   Acknowledgements: 'A thank you' from the BRC

The BRC wishes to acknowledge all those food industry experts who have contributed to the preparation of the *Global Standard for Food Safety* Issue 6. A list of those who participated in this review is detailed in Appendix 10.

2   The Food Safety Management System

2.1   Principles of the *Global Standard for Food Safety*

A food business must have a full understanding of the products produced, manufactured and distributed, and have systems in place to identify and control hazards significant to the safety of food. The *Global Standard for Food Safety* is based on two key components: senior management commitment and HACCP (Hazard Analysis Critical Control Point – a step-by-step approach to managing food safety risks).

2.1.1   Senior management commitment

Within a food business, food safety must be seen as a cross-functional responsibility that includes activities that draw on many departments, using different skills and levels of management expertise across the organisation. Effective food safety management extends beyond technical departments and must involve commitment from production operations, engineering, distribution management, procurement of raw materials, customer feedback and human resource activity such as training.

The starting point for an effective food safety plan is the commitment of senior management to the development of an all-encompassing policy as a means to guide the activities that collectively assure food safety. The *Global Standard for Food Safety* places a high priority on clear evidence of senior management commitment.

2.1.2   A HACCP based system

The *Global Standard for Food Safety* requires the development of a food safety plan based on HACCP. The development of the plan requires the input of all relevant departments and must be supported by senior management.

2.2　The format of the *Global Standard for Food Safety*

The *Global Standard for Food Safety* requires the development of and compliance with the following:

- *Senior management commitment.* The resources required for demonstration of commitment to achieving the requirements of the Standard are detailed in Section II, Part 1.

- *A HACCP plan.* This provides a focus on the significant product and process food safety hazards that require specific control to assure the safety of individual food products or lines as detailed in Section II, Part 2.

- *A quality management system.* Details of the organisational and management policies and procedures that provide a framework by which the organisation will achieve the requirements in this Standard as given in Section II, Part 3.

- *Pre-requisite programmes.* The basic environmental and operational conditions in a food business that are necessary for the production of safe food. These control generic hazards covering Good Manufacturing and Good Hygienic Practice as detailed in Section II, Parts 4–7.

SECTION II

REQUIREMENTS

Section II

Requirements

Introduction to the Requirements

The format of the Standard

Each clause of the Standard begins with a highlighted paragraph in bold text to signify the statement of intent. This sets out the expected outcome of compliance with the particular clause. This forms part of the audit and all companies must comply with the statement of intent.

Below this 'statement of intent' are requirements in a tabular format, which set out in more specific detail requirements which, if applied appropriately, will help to achieve the stated objective of the clause. All of the requirements shall form part of the audit and must be complied with in order for a certificate to be issued.

Colour coding of requirements

There is a choice of audit protocols available for undertaking audits and certification against this Standard. Audits may be undertaken in a single visit (as either an unannounced or announced audit), or sites may opt for the split audit option, where the first part of the audit (part 1) is unannounced and concentrates on good manufacturing practices (GMP) and there is a later, scheduled, announced audit (part 2) reviewing primarily records and procedures.

The audit requirements within the Standard have been colour coded to provide a guide as to which requirements would be expected to be covered on part 1 and part 2 audits where this audit option is selected. The colour coding also helps to identify the requirements which would usually be expected to be audited as part of the assessment of the production areas and facilities or would form part of such an audit trail initiated in the factory.

Key to colour coding of requirements

Requirements assessed on part 1 - audit of good manufacturing practice		
Requirements assessed on part 2 – audit of records, systems and documentation		
Requirements assessed on both part 1 and part 2		

Fundamental requirements

Within the Standard certain requirements have been designated as 'fundamental' requirements, which are marked with the word 'FUNDAMENTAL' immediately after the section heading and denoted with the following symbol ⊙. These requirements relate to systems that are crucial to the establishment and operation of an effective food quality and safety operation. The clauses deemed fundamental are:

- Senior management commitment and continual improvement, Clause 1.1
- The food safety plan – HACCP, Clause 2
- Internal audits, Clause 3.4
- Corrective action, Clause 3.7
- Traceability, Clause 3.9

■   Layout, product flow and segregation, Clause 4.3

■   Housekeeping and hygiene, Clause 4.11

■   Management of allergens, Clause 5.2

■   Control of operations, Clause 6.1

■   Training, Clause 7.1.

Failure to comply with the statement of intent of a fundamental clause (i.e. a major non-conformity), leads to non-certification at an initial audit or withdrawal of certification at subsequent audits. This will require a further full audit to establish demonstrable evidence of compliance.

Senior Management Commitment

1.1 Senior management commitment and continual improvement

FUNDAMENTAL

The company's senior management shall demonstrate they are fully committed to the implementation of the requirements of the *Global Standard for Food Safety* and to processes which facilitate continual improvement of food safety and quality management.

Clause	Requirements
1.1.1	The company shall have a documented policy which states the company's intention to meet its obligation to produce safe and legal products to the specified quality and its responsibility to its customers. This shall be: ⬤ signed by the person with overall responsibility for the site ⬤ communicated to all staff.
1.1.2	The company's senior management shall ensure that clear objectives are defined to maintain and improve the safety, legality and quality of products manufactured, in accordance with the quality policy and this Standard. These objectives shall be: ⬤ documented and include targets or clear measures of success ⬤ clearly communicated to relevant staff ⬤ monitored and results reported at least quarterly to site senior management.
1.1.3	Management review meetings attended by the site's senior management shall be undertaken at appropriate planned intervals, annually as a minimum, to review the site performance against the Standard and objectives set in 1.1.2. The review process shall include the evaluation of: ⬤ previous management review action plans and time frames ⬤ results of internal, second party and/or third party audits ⬤ customer complaints and results of any customer performance reviews ⬤ incidents, corrective actions, out of specification results and non-conforming materials ⬤ review of the management of the HACCP system ⬤ resource requirements. Records of the meeting shall be documented and used to revise the objectives. The decisions and actions agreed within the review process shall be effectively communicated to appropriate staff, and actions implemented within agreed time scales.
1.1.4	The company shall have a demonstrable meeting programme which enables food safety, legality and quality issues to be brought to the attention of senior management at least monthly and allows for the resolution of issues requiring immediate action.
1.1.5	The company's senior management shall provide the human and financial resources required to produce food safely in compliance with the requirements of this Standard and for the implementation of the HACCP-based food safety plan.

Clause	Requirements
1.1.6	The company's senior management shall have a system in place to ensure that the company is kept informed of scientific and technical developments, industry codes of practice and all relevant legislation applicable in the country of raw material supply, production and, where known, the country where the product will be sold.
1.1.7	The company shall have a genuine, original hard copy or electronic version of the current Standard available.
1.1.8	Where the company is certificated to the Standard it shall ensure that announced recertification audits occur on or before the audit due date indicated on the certificate.
1.1.9	The most senior production or operations manager on site shall attend the opening and closing meetings of the audit for *Global Standard for Food Safety* certification. Relevant departmental managers or their deputies shall be available as required during the audit process.
1.1.10	The company's senior management shall ensure that the root causes of non-conformities identified at the previous audit against the Standard have been effectively addressed to prevent recurrence.

1.2   Organisational structure, responsibilities and management authority

The company shall have a clear organisational structure and lines of communication to enable effective management of product safety, legality and quality.

Clause	Requirements
1.2.1	The company shall have an organisation chart demonstrating the management structure of the company. The responsibilities for the management of activities which ensure food safety, legality and quality shall be clearly allocated and understood by the managers responsible. It shall be clearly documented who deputises in the absence of the responsible person.
1.2.2	The company's senior management shall ensure that all employees are aware of their responsibilities. Where documented work instructions exist for activities undertaken, the relevant employees shall have access to these and be able to demonstrate that work is carried out in accordance with the instruction.

The Food Safety Plan – HACCP

FUNDAMENTAL

The company shall have a fully implemented and effective food safety plan based on Codex Alimentarius HACCP principles.

2.1   The HACCP food safety team – Codex Alimentarius Step 1

Clause	Requirements
2.1.1	The HACCP plan shall be developed and managed by a multi-disciplinary food safety team that includes those responsible for quality/technical, production operations, engineering and other relevant functions. The team leader shall have an in-depth knowledge of HACCP and be able to demonstrate competence and experience. The team members shall have specific knowledge of HACCP and relevant knowledge of product, process and associated hazards. In the event of the company not having appropriate in-house knowledge, external expertise may be used, but day-to-day management of the food safety system shall remain the responsibility of the company.

2.2   Prerequisite programmes

Clause		Requirements
2.2.1		The company shall establish and maintain environmental and operational programmes necessary to create an environment suitable to produce safe and legal food products (prerequisite programmes). As a guide these may include the following, although this is not an exhaustive list: ● cleaning and sanitising ● pest control ● maintenance programmes for equipment and buildings ● personal hygiene requirements ● staff training ● purchasing ● transportation arrangements ● processes to prevent cross-contamination ● allergen controls. The control measures and monitoring procedures for the prerequisite programmes must be clearly documented and shall be included within the development and reviews of the HACCP programme.

2.3   Describe the product – Codex Alimentarius Step 2

Clause	Requirements
2.3.1	The scope of each HACCP plan, including the products and processes covered, shall be defined. For each product or group of products a full description shall be developed, which includes all relevant information on food safety. As a guide, this may include the following, although this is not an exhaustive list:
	● composition, e.g. raw materials, ingredients, allergens, recipe
	● origin of ingredients
	● physical or chemical properties that impact food safety, e.g. pH, a_w
	● treatment and processing, e.g. cooking, cooling
	● packaging system, e.g. modified atmosphere, vacuum
	● storage and distribution conditions, e.g. chilled, ambient
	● target safe shelf life under prescribed storage and usage conditions
	● instructions for use, and potential for known customer misuse, e.g. storage, preparation.
2.3.2	All relevant information needed to conduct the hazard analysis shall be collected, maintained, documented and updated. The company will ensure that the HACCP plan is based on comprehensive information sources, which are referenced and available on request. As a guide, this may include the following, although this is not an exhaustive list:
	● the latest scientific literature
	● historical and known hazards associated with specific food products
	● relevant codes of practice
	● recognised guidelines
	● food safety legislation relevant for the production and sale of products
	● customer requirements.

2.4   Identify intended use – Codex Alimentarius Step 3

Clause	Requirements
2.4.1	The intended use of the product by the customer shall be described, defining the consumer target groups, including the suitability of the product for vulnerable groups of the population (e.g. infants, elderly, allergy sufferers).

2.5   Construct a process flow diagram – Codex Alimentarius Step 4

Clause	Requirements
2.5.1	A flow diagram shall be prepared to cover each product, product category or process. This shall set out all aspects of the food process operation within the HACCP scope, from raw material receipt through to processing, storage and distribution. As a guide, this should include the following, although this is not an exhaustive list: <ul><li>plan of premises and equipment layout</li><li>raw materials including introduction of utilities and other contact materials, e.g. water, packaging</li><li>sequence and interaction of all process steps</li><li>outsourced processes and subcontracted work</li><li>process parameters</li><li>potential for process delay</li><li>rework and recycling</li><li>low/**high-care/high-risk** area segregation</li><li>finished products, intermediate/semi-processed products, by-products and waste.</li></ul>

2.6   Verify flow diagram – Codex Alimentarius Step 5

Clause	Requirements
2.6.1	The HACCP food safety team shall verify the accuracy of the flow diagrams by on-site audit and challenge at least annually. Daily and seasonal variations shall be considered and evaluated. Records of verification of flow diagrams shall be maintained.

2.7 List all potential hazards associated with each process step, conduct a hazard analysis and consider any measures to control identified hazards – Codex Alimentarius Step 6, Principle 1

Clause	Requirements
2.7.1	The HACCP food safety team shall identify and record all the potential hazards that are reasonably expected to occur at each step in relation to product, process and facilities. This shall include hazards present in raw materials, those introduced during the process or surviving the process steps, and allergen risks (refer to clause 5.2). It shall also take account of the preceding and following steps in the process chain.
2.7.2	The HACCP food safety team shall conduct a hazard analysis to identify hazards which need to be prevented, eliminated or reduced to acceptable levels. Consideration shall be given to the following: ● likely occurrence of hazard ● severity of the effects on consumer safety ● vulnerability of those exposed ● survival and multiplication of micro-organisms of specific concern to the product ● presence or production of toxins, chemicals or foreign bodies ● contamination of raw materials, intermediate/semi-processed product, or finished product. Where elimination of the hazard is not practical, justification for acceptable levels of the hazard in the finished product shall be determined and documented.
2.7.3	The HACCP food safety team shall consider the control measures necessary to prevent or eliminate a food safety hazard or reduce it to an acceptable level. Where the control is achieved through existing prerequisite programmes, this shall be stated and the adequacy of the programme to control the hazard validated. Consideration may be given to using more than one control measure.

2.8 Determine the critical control points (CCP) – Codex Alimentarius Step 7, Principle 2

Clause	Requirements
2.8.1	For each hazard that requires control, control points shall be reviewed to identify those that are critical. This requires a logical approach and may be facilitated by use of a decision tree. CCPs shall be those control points which are required in order to prevent or eliminate a food safety hazard or reduce it to an acceptable level. If a hazard is identified at a step where control is necessary for safety but the control does not exist, the product or process shall be modified at that step, or at an earlier or later step, to provide a control measure.

50029983

2.9 Establish critical limits for each CCP – Codex Alimentarius Step 8, Principle 3

Clause	Requirements
2.9.1	For each CCP, the appropriate critical limits shall be defined in order to identify clearly whether the process is in or out of control. Critical limits shall be: ● measurable wherever possible, e.g. time, temperature, pH ● supported by clear guidance or examples where measures are subjective, e.g. photographs.
2.9.2	The HACCP food safety team shall validate each CCP. Documented evidence shall show that the control measures selected and critical limits identified are capable of consistently controlling the hazard to the specified acceptable level.

2.10 Establish a monitoring system for each CCP – Codex Alimentarius Step 9, Principle 4

Clause		Requirements
2.10.1		A monitoring procedure shall be established for each CCP to ensure compliance with critical limits. The monitoring system shall be able to detect loss of control of CCPs and wherever possible provide information in time for corrective action to be taken. As a guide, consideration may be given to the following, although this is not an exhaustive list: ● online measurement ● offline measurement ● continuous measurement, e.g. thermographs, pH meters etc. ● where discontinuous measurement is used, the system shall ensure that the sample taken is representative of the batch of product.
2.10.2		Records associated with the monitoring of each CCP shall include the date, time and result of measurement and shall be signed by the person responsible for the monitoring and verified, as appropriate, by an authorised person. Where records are in electronic form there shall be evidence that records have been checked and verified.

2.11 Establish a corrective action plan – Codex Alimentarius Step 10, Principle 5

Clause	Requirements
2.11.1	The HACCP food safety team shall specify and document the corrective action to be taken when monitored results indicate a failure to meet a control limit, or when monitored results indicate a trend towards loss of control. This shall include the action to be taken by nominated personnel with regard to any products that have been manufactured during the period when the process was out of control.

2.12   Establish verification procedures – Codex Alimentarius Step 11, Principle 6

Clause	Requirements
2.12.1	Procedures of verification shall be established to confirm that the HACCP plan, including controls managed by prerequisite programmes, are effective. Examples of verification activities include: ● internal audits ● review of records where acceptable limits have been exceeded ● review of complaints by enforcement authorities or customers ● review of incidents of product withdrawal or recall. Results of verification shall be recorded and communicated to the HACCP food safety team.

2.13   HACCP documentation and record keeping – Codex Alimentarius Step 12, Principle 7

Clause	Requirements
2.13.1	Documentation and record keeping shall be sufficient to enable the company to verify that the HACCP controls, including controls managed by prerequisite programmes, are in place and maintained.

2.14   Review the HACCP plan

Clause	Requirements
2.14.1	The HACCP food safety team shall review the HACCP plan and prerequisite programmes at least annually and prior to any changes which may affect product safety. As a guide, these may include the following, although this is not an exhaustive list: ● change in raw materials or supplier of raw materials ● change in ingredients/recipe ● change in processing conditions or equipment ● change in packaging, storage or distribution conditions ● change in consumer use ● emergence of a new risk, for example adulteration of an ingredient ● developments in scientific information associated with ingredients, process or product. Appropriate changes resulting from the review shall be incorporated into the HACCP plan and/or prerequisite programmes, fully documented and validation recorded.

S0029783

3   Food safety and quality management system

3.1   Food safety and quality manual

The company's processes and procedures to meet the requirements of this Standard shall be documented to allow consistent application, facilitate training, and support due diligence in the production of a safe product.

Clause	Requirements
3.1.1	The company's documented procedures, working methods and practices shall be collated in the form of a printed or electronic quality manual.
3.1.2	The food safety and quality manual shall be fully implemented and the manual or relevant components shall be readily available to key staff.
3.1.3	All procedures and work instructions shall be clearly legible, unambiguous, in appropriate languages and sufficiently detailed to enable their correct application by appropriate staff. This shall include the use of photographs, diagrams or other pictorial instructions where written communication alone is not sufficient (e.g. there are issues of literacy or foreign language).

3.2   Documentation control

The company shall operate an effective document control system to ensure that only the correct versions of documents, including recording forms, are available and in use.

Clause	Requirements
3.2.1	The company shall have a procedure to manage documents which form part of the food safety and quality system. This shall include: • a list of all controlled documents indicating the latest version number • the method for the identification and authorisation of controlled documents • a record of the reason for any changes or amendments to documents • the system for the replacement of existing documents when these are updated.

3.3   Record completion and maintenance

The company shall maintain genuine records to demonstrate the effective control of product safety, legality and quality.

Clause	Requirements
3.3.1	Records shall be legible, retained in good condition and retrievable. Any alterations to records shall be authorised and justification for alteration shall be recorded. Where records are in electronic form these shall be suitably backed up to prevent loss.
3.3.2	Records shall be retained for a defined period with consideration given to any legal or customer requirements and to the shelf life of the product. This shall take into account, where it is specified on the label, the possibility that shelf life may be extended by the consumer (e.g. by freezing). As a minimum, records shall be retained for the shelf life of the product plus 12 months.

3.4   Internal audit

FUNDAMENTAL

The company shall be able to demonstrate it verifies the effective application of the food safety plan and the implementation of the requirements of the *Global Standard for Food Safety.*

Clause	Requirements
3.4.1	There shall be a planned programme of internal audits with a scope which covers the implementation of the HACCP programme, prerequisite programmes and procedures implemented to achieve this Standard. The scope and frequency of the audits shall be established in relation to the risks associated with the activity and previous audit performance; all activities shall be covered at least annually.
3.4.2	Internal audits shall be carried out by appropriately trained competent auditors, who are independent from the audited department.
3.4.3	The internal audit programme shall be fully implemented. Internal audit reports shall identify conformity as well as non-conformity and the results shall be reported to the personnel responsible for the activity audited. Corrective actions and timescales for their implementation shall be agreed and completion of the actions verified.
3.4.4	In addition to the internal audit programme there shall be a programme of documented inspections to ensure that the factory environment and processing equipment is maintained in a suitable condition for food production. These inspections shall include: ● hygiene inspections to assess cleaning and housekeeping performance ● fabrication inspections to identify risks to the product from the building or equipment. The frequency of these inspections shall be based on risk but will be no less than once per month in open product areas.

3.5 Supplier and raw material approval and performance monitoring

3.5.1 Management of suppliers of raw materials and packaging

The company shall have an effective supplier approval and monitoring system to ensure that any potential risks from raw materials (including packaging) to the safety, legality and quality of the final product are understood and managed.

Clause	Requirements
3.5.1.1	The company shall undertake a documented risk assessment of each raw material or group of raw materials to identify potential risks to product safety, legality and quality. This shall take into account the potential for: ○ allergen contamination ○ foreign body risks ○ microbiological contamination ○ chemical contamination. Consideration shall also be given to the significance of a raw material to the quality of the final product. The risk assessment shall form the basis for the raw material acceptance and testing procedure and for the processes adopted for supplier approval and monitoring.
3.5.1.2	The company shall have a documented supplier approval and ongoing monitoring procedure to ensure that suppliers are manufacturing products under hygienic conditions, effectively manage risks to raw material quality and safety and are operating effective traceability processes. The approval and monitoring procedure shall be based on one or a combination of: ○ supplier audits ○ third party audits or certification, e.g. to BRC Global Standards ○ supplier questionnaires. Where approval is based on questionnaires, these shall be reissued at least every three years and suppliers required to notify the site of any significant changes in the interim.
3.5.1.3	The procedures shall define how exceptions are handled (e.g. where raw material suppliers are prescribed by a customer or where products are purchased from agents and direct audit or monitoring has not been undertaken).

3.5.2   Raw material and packaging acceptance and monitoring procedures

Controls on the acceptance of raw materials shall ensure that raw materials do not compromise the safety, legality or quality of products.

Clause	Requirements
3.5.2.1	The company shall have a documented procedure for the acceptance of raw materials and packaging on receipt based upon the risk assessment (3.5.1). Raw material acceptance and its release for use shall be based on one or a combination of: ● visual inspection on receipt ● certificates of conformance – specific to each consignment ● certificates of analysis ● product sampling and testing. A list of raw materials and the requirements to be met for acceptance shall be available. The parameters for acceptance and frequency of testing shall be clearly defined.
3.5.2.2	The procedures shall be fully implemented and records maintained to demonstrate the basis for acceptance of each batch of raw materials.

3.5.3   Management of suppliers of services

The company shall be able to demonstrate that where services are outsourced, the service is appropriate and any risks presented to food safety have been evaluated to ensure effective controls are in place.

Clause	Requirements
3.5.3.1	There shall be a documented procedure for the approval and monitoring of suppliers of services. Such services shall include as appropriate: ● pest control ● laundry services ● contracted cleaning ● contracted servicing and maintenance of equipment ● transport and distribution ● off-site storage of ingredients, packaging or products ● laboratory testing ● catering services ● waste management.
3.5.3.2	Contracts or formal agreements shall exist with the suppliers of services which clearly define service expectations and ensure potential food safety risks associated with the service have been addressed.

3.5.4   Management of outsourced processing

Where any intermediate process steps in the manufacture of a product which is included within the scope of certification is subcontracted to a third party or undertaken at another company site, this shall be managed to ensure this does not compromise the safety, legality or quality of the product.

Clause	Requirements
3.5.4.1	The company shall be able to demonstrate that where part of the production process is outsourced and undertaken off site, this has been declared to the brand owner and, where required, approval granted.
3.5.4.2	The company shall ensure that subcontractors are approved and monitored by successful completion of either a documented site audit or third-party certification to the BRC *Global Standard for Food Safety* or other GFSI-recognised Standard (see Glossary).
3.5.4.3	Any outsourced processing operations shall: ● be undertaken in accordance with established contracts which clearly define any processing requirements and product specification ● maintain product traceability.
3.5.4.4	The company shall establish inspection and test procedures for outsourced product on return, including visual, chemical and/or microbiological testing, dependent on risk assessment.

3.6   Specifications

Specifications shall exist for raw materials including packaging, finished products and any product or service which could affect the integrity of the finished product.

Clause	Requirements
3.6.1	Specifications for raw materials and packaging shall be adequate and accurate and ensure compliance with relevant safety and legislative requirements. The specifications shall include defined limits for relevant attributes of the material which may affect the quality or safety of the final products (e.g. chemical, microbiological or physical standards).
3.6.2	Manufacturing instructions and process specifications shall comply with recipes and quality criteria as detailed in agreed customer specifications.
3.6.3	Specifications shall be available for all finished products. These shall either be in the agreed format of the customer or, in the case of branded products, include key data to meet legal requirements and assist the customer in the safe usage of the product.
3.6.4	The company shall seek formal agreement of specifications with relevant parties. Where specifications are not formally agreed then the company shall be able to demonstrate that it has taken steps to ensure formal agreement is in place.
3.6.5	Specifications shall be reviewed whenever products change (e.g. ingredients, processing method) or at least every three years. The date of review and the approval of any changes shall be recorded.

3.7   Corrective action

FUNDAMENTAL

The company shall be able to demonstrate that they use the information from identified failures in the food safety and quality management system to make necessary corrections and prevent recurrence.

Clause	Requirements
3.7.1	The company shall have a documented procedure for handling non-conformances identified within the scope of this Standard to include: ● clear documentation of the non-conformity ● assessment of consequences by a suitably competent and authorised person ● identification of the corrective action to address the immediate issue ● identification of an appropriate timescale for correction ● identification of personnel with appropriate authority responsible for corrective action ● verification that the corrective action has been implemented and is effective ● identification of the root cause of the non-conformity and implementation of any necessary corrective action.

3.8   Control of non-conforming product

The company shall ensure that any out-of-specification product is effectively managed to prevent release.

Clause	Requirements
3.8.1	There shall be documented procedures for managing non-conforming products which include: ● the requirement for staff to identify and report potentially non-conforming product ● clear identification of non-conforming product, e.g. direct labelling or the use of IT systems ● secure storage to prevent accidental release, e.g. isolation areas ● referral to the brand owner where required ● defined responsibilities for decision making on the use or disposal of products appropriate to the issue, e.g. destruction, reworking, downgrading to an alternative label or acceptance by concession ● records of the decision on the use or disposal of the product ● records of destruction where product is destroyed for food safety reasons.

3.9   Traceability

FUNDAMENTAL

The company shall be able to trace all raw material product lots (including packaging) from their supplier through all stages of processing and despatch to their customer and vice versa.

Clause	Requirements
3.9.1	Identification of raw materials, including primary and any other relevant packaging and processing aids, intermediate/semi-processed products, part-used materials, finished products and materials pending investigation, shall be adequate to ensure traceability.
3.9.2	The company shall test the traceability system across the range of product groups to ensure traceability can be determined from raw material to finished product and vice versa, including quantity check/mass balance. This shall occur at a predetermined frequency and results shall be retained for inspection. The test shall take place at least annually. Full traceability should be achievable within four hours.
3.9.3	Where rework or any reworking operation is performed, traceability shall be maintained.

3.10   Complaint handling

Customer complaints shall be handled effectively and information used to reduce recurring complaint levels.

Clause	Requirements
3.10.1	All complaints shall be recorded, investigated and the results of the investigation and root cause of the issue recorded where sufficient information is provided. Actions appropriate to the seriousness and frequency of the problems identified shall be carried out promptly and effectively by appropriately trained staff.
3.10.2	Complaint data shall be analysed for significant trends and used to implement ongoing improvements to product safety, legality and quality, and to avoid recurrence. This analysis shall be made available to relevant staff.

3.11   Management of incidents, product withdrawal and product recall

The company shall have a plan and system in place to effectively manage incidents and enable the effective withdrawal and recall of products should this be required.

Clause	Requirements
3.11.1	The company shall have documented procedures designed to report and effectively manage incidents and potential emergency situations that impact food safety, legality or quality. This shall include consideration of contingency plans to maintain business continuity. Incidents may include: • disruption to key services such as water, energy, transport, refrigeration processes, staff availability and communications • events such as fire, flood or natural disaster • malicious contamination or sabotage. Where products which have been released from the site may be affected by an incident, consideration shall be given to the need to withdraw or recall products.
3.11.2	The company shall have a documented product withdrawal and recall procedure. This shall include as a minimum: • identification of key personnel constituting the recall management team, with clearly identified responsibilities • guidelines for deciding whether a product needs to be recalled or withdrawn and the records to be maintained • an up-to-date list of key contacts or reference to the location of such a list, e.g. recall management team, emergency services, suppliers, customers, Certification Body, regulatory authority • a communication plan including the provision of information to customers, consumers and regulatory authorities in a timely manner • details of external agencies providing advice and support as necessary, e.g. specialist laboratories, regulatory authority and legal expertise • a plan to handle the logistics of product traceability, recovery or disposal of affected product and stock reconciliation. The procedure shall be capable of being operated at any time.
3.11.3	The product recall and withdrawal procedures shall be tested, at least annually, in a way that ensures their effective operation. Results of the test shall be retained and shall include timings of key activities. The results of the test and of any actual recall shall be used to review the procedure and implement improvements as necessary.
3.11.4	In the event of a product recall, the Certification Body issuing the current certificate for the site against this Standard shall be informed within three working days of the decision to issue a recall.

Site Standards

4.1 External standards

The production site shall be of suitable size, location, construction and design to reduce the risk of contamination and facilitate the production of safe and legal finished products.

Clause	Requirements
4.1.1	Consideration shall be given to local activities and the site environment, which may have an adverse impact on finished product integrity, and measures shall be taken to prevent contamination. Where measures have been put into place to protect the site (from potential contaminants, flooding etc.), they shall be reviewed in response to any changes.
4.1.2	The external areas shall be maintained in good order. Where buildings are surrounded by grassed or planted areas, they shall be regularly tended and well-maintained. External traffic routes under site control shall be suitably surfaced and maintained in good repair to avoid contamination of the product.
4.1.3	The building fabric shall be maintained to minimise potential for product contamination (e.g. elimination of bird roosting sites, sealing gaps around pipes to prevent pest entry, ingress of water and other contaminants).

4.2 Security

Security systems shall ensure that products are protected from theft or malicious contamination whilst under the control of the site.

Clause	Requirements
4.2.1	The company shall undertake a documented assessment of the security arrangements and potential risks to the products from any deliberate attempt to inflict contamination or damage. Areas shall be assessed according to risk; sensitive or restricted areas shall be defined, clearly marked, monitored and controlled. Identified security arrangements shall be implemented and reviewed at least annually.
4.2.2	Measures shall be in place to ensure only authorised personnel have access to production and storage areas and access to the site by employees, contractors and visitors shall be controlled. A visitor reporting system shall be in place. Staff shall be trained in site security procedures and encouraged to report unidentified or unknown visitors.
4.2.3	Where required by legislation, the site shall be registered with, or be approved by, the appropriate authority.

4.3   Layout, product flow and segregation

FUNDAMENTAL

The factory layout, flow of processes and movement of personnel shall be sufficient to prevent the risk of product contamination and to comply with relevant legislation.

Clause	Requirements
4.3.1	There shall be a plan of the site which designates areas where product is at different levels of risk from contamination; that is: ● enclosed product areas ● low-risk areas ● high-care areas ● high-risk areas. See Appendix 2 for guidance. This shall be taken into account when determining the prerequisite programmes for the particular areas of the site.
4.3.2	The site plan shall define: ● access points for personnel and travel routes ● location of staff facilities and routes to the facilities from places of work ● production process flow ● routes for the removal of waste ● routes for the movement of rework. If it is necessary to allow access through production areas, designated walkways shall be provided that ensure there is adequate segregation from materials. All facilities shall be designed and positioned, where possible, so that movement of personnel is by simple, logical routes. The movement of waste and rework shall not compromise the safety of products.
4.3.3	Contractors and visitors, including drivers, shall be made aware of all procedures for access to premises and the requirements of the areas they are visiting, with special reference to hazards and potential product contamination. Contractors involved in maintenance or repair activities shall be under the supervision of a nominated person.
4.3.4	In low-risk areas the process flow together with the use of demonstrably effective procedures shall be in place to minimise the risk of the contamination of raw materials, intermediate/semi-processed products, packaging and finished products.
4.3.5	Where **high-care areas** are part of the manufacturing site there should be physical segregation between these areas and other parts of the site. Segregation shall take into account the flow of product, nature of materials, equipment, personnel, waste, airflow, air quality and utilities provision. Where physical barriers are not in place, the site shall have undertaken a full evaluation of the risks of cross-contamination and alternative effective processes shall be in place to protect products from contamination.
4.3.6	Where **high-risk areas** are part of the manufacturing site, there shall be physical segregation between these areas and other parts of the site. Segregation shall take into account the flow of product, nature of materials, equipment, personnel, waste, airflow, air quality and utilities provision. The location of transfer points shall not compromise the segregation between high-risk areas and other areas of the factory. Practices shall be in place to minimise risk of product contamination (e.g. the disinfection of materials on entry).

Clause	Requirements
4.3.7	Premises shall allow sufficient working space and storage capacity to enable all operations to be carried out properly under safe hygienic conditions.
4.3.8	Temporary structures constructed during building work or refurbishment, etc. shall be designed and located to avoid pest harbourage and ensure the safety and quality of products.

4.4   Building fabric

Raw material handling, preparation, processing, packing and storage areas

The fabrication of the site, buildings and facilities shall be suitable for the intended purpose.

Clause	Requirements
4.4.1	**Walls** shall be constructed, finished and maintained to prevent the accumulation of dirt, minimise condensation and mould growth, and facilitate cleaning.
4.4.2	**Floors** shall be suitably hard wearing to meet the demands of the process, and withstand cleaning materials and methods. They shall be impervious and maintained in good repair.
4.4.3	**Drainage**, where provided, shall be sited, designed and maintained to minimise risk of product contamination and not compromise product safety. Machinery and piping shall be arranged so that, wherever feasible, process waste water goes directly to drain. Where significant amounts of water are used, or direct piping to drain is not feasible, floors shall have adequate falls to cope with the flow of any water or effluent towards suitable drainage.
4.4.4	Where sites include **high-care** or **high-risk** facilities, there shall be a plan of the drains for these areas which shows the direction of flow and location of any equipment fitted to prevent the back up of waste water. The flow of drains shall not present a risk of contamination of the high-care/risk area.
4.4.5	**Ceilings and overheads** shall be constructed, finished and maintained to prevent the risk of product contamination.
4.4.6	Where **suspended ceilings** or roof voids are present, adequate access to the void shall be provided to facilitate inspection for pest activity, unless the void is fully sealed.
4.4.7	Where there is a risk to product, **windows**, and roof glazing which is designed to be opened for ventilation purposes, shall be adequately screened to prevent the ingress of pests.
4.4.8	Where they pose a risk to product, glass windows shall be protected against breakage.
4.4.9	**Doors** shall be maintained in good condition. External doors and dock levellers shall be close fitting or adequately proofed. External doors to open product areas shall not be opened during production periods except in emergencies. Where external doors to enclosed product areas are opened, suitable precautions shall be taken to prevent pest ingress.
4.4.10	Suitable and sufficient **lighting** shall be provided for correct operation of processes, inspection of product and effective cleaning.
4.4.11	Where they constitute a risk to product, bulbs and strip lights – including those on electric fly-killer devices – shall be adequately protected. Where full protection cannot be provided, alternative management such as wire mesh screens or monitoring procedures shall be in place.
4.4.12	Adequate **ventilation** and **extraction** shall be provided in product storage and processing environments to prevent condensation or excessive dust.
4.4.13	**High-risk areas** shall be supplied with sufficient changes of filtered air. The filter specification used and frequency of air changes shall be documented. This shall be based on a risk assessment, taking into account the source of the air and the requirement to maintain a positive air pressure relative to the surrounding areas.

4.5   Utilities – water, ice, air and other gases

Utilities used within the production and storage areas shall be monitored to effectively control the risk of product contamination.

Clause	Requirements
4.5.1	All water used as a raw material in the manufacture of processed food, the preparation of product, or for equipment or plant cleaning shall be supplied in sufficient quantity, be potable at point of use or pose no risk of contamination according to applicable legislation. The microbiological and chemical quality of water shall be analysed at least annually. The sampling points and frequency of analysis shall be based on risk, taking into account the source of the water, on-site storage and distribution facilities, previous sample history and usage.
4.5.2	An up-to-date plan shall be available of the water distribution system on site, including holding tanks, water treatment and water recycling as appropriate. The plan shall be used as a basis for water sampling and the management of water quality.
4.5.3	Where legislation specifically permits the use of water which may not be potable for initial product cleaning (e.g. for the storage/washing of fish), the water shall meet the designated legal requirement for this operation.
4.5.4	Air, other gases and steam used directly in contact with or as an ingredient in products shall be monitored to ensure this does not represent a contamination risk. Compressed air used directly in contact with the product shall be filtered.

4.6   Equipment

All food processing equipment shall be suitable for the intended purpose and shall be used to minimise the risk of contamination of product.

Clause	Requirements
4.6.1	All equipment shall be constructed of appropriate materials. The design and placement of equipment shall ensure it can be effectively cleaned and maintained.
4.6.2	Equipment which is in direct contact with food shall be suitable for food contact and meet legal requirements where applicable.

4.7   Maintenance

An effective maintenance programme shall be in operation for plant and equipment to prevent contamination and reduce the potential for breakdowns.

Clause	Requirements
4.7.1	There shall be a documented planned maintenance schedule or condition monitoring system which includes all plant and processing equipment. The maintenance requirements shall be defined when commissioning new equipment.
4.7.2	In addition to any planned maintenance programme, where there is a risk of product contamination by foreign bodies arising from equipment damage, the equipment shall be inspected at predetermined intervals, inspection results documented and appropriate action taken.
4.7.3	Where temporary repairs are made, these shall be controlled to ensure the safety or legality of product is not jeopardised. These temporary measures shall be permanently repaired as soon as practicable and within a defined timescale.
4.7.4	The company shall ensure that the safety or legality of product is not jeopardised during maintenance and subsequent cleaning operations. Maintenance work shall be followed by a documented hygiene clearance procedure, which records that product contamination hazards have been removed from machinery and equipment.
4.7.5	Materials used for equipment and plant maintenance and that pose a risk by direct or indirect contact with raw materials, intermediate and finished products, such as lubricating oil, shall be food grade.
4.7.6	Engineering workshops shall be kept clean and tidy and controls shall be in place to prevent contamination risks to the product (e.g. provision of swarf mats at the entrance/exit of workshops).

4.8   Staff facilities

Staff facilities shall be sufficient to accommodate the required number of personnel, and shall be designed and operated to minimise the risk of product contamination. The facilities shall be maintained in good and clean condition.

Clause	Requirements
4.8.1	Designated changing facilities shall be provided for all personnel, whether staff, visitor or contractor. These shall be sited to allow direct access to the production, packing or storage areas without recourse to any external area. Where this is not possible, a risk assessment shall be carried out and procedures implemented accordingly (e.g. the provision of cleaning facilities for footwear).
4.8.2	Storage facilities of sufficient size to accommodate personal items shall be provided for all personnel who work in raw material handling, preparation, processing, packing and storage areas.
4.8.3	Outdoor clothing and other personal items shall be stored separately from workwear within the changing facilities. Facilities shall be available to separate clean and dirty workwear.

Clause	Requirements
4.8.4	Where an operation includes a **high-care area**, personnel shall enter via a specially designated changing facility with arrangements to ensure that protective clothing will not be contaminated before entry to the high-care area. The changing facilities shall incorporate the following requirements: ● clear instructions for the order of changing into dedicated protective clothes to prevent the contamination of clean clothing ● dedicated footwear, by exception shoe coverings shall be provided for visitors only to be worn in the high-care area ● an effective system shall be provided to segregate areas for wearing high-care from other footwear (e.g. a barrier or bench system) or there shall be an effective boot wash on entrance to the high-care area ● protective clothing shall be visually distinctive from that worn in lower risk areas and shall not be worn outside of the high-care area ● hand-washing during the changing procedure shall be incorporated to prevent contamination of the clean protective clothing ● on entry to high-care areas, hand-washing and disinfection shall be provided.
4.8.5	Where an operation includes a **high-risk area**, personnel shall enter via a specially designated changing facility at the entrance to the high-risk area. The changing facilities shall include the following requirements: ● clear instructions for the order of changing into dedicated protective clothes to prevent the contamination of clean clothing ● dedicated footwear shall be provided to be worn in the high-risk area ● an effective system shall be provided to segregate areas for wearing high-risk and other footwear, e.g. a barrier or bench system ● protective clothing shall be visually distinctive from that worn in other areas and shall not be worn outside of the high-risk area ● hand-washing during the changing procedure shall be incorporated to prevent contamination of the clean protective clothing ● on entry to high-risk areas, hand-washing and disinfection shall be provided.
4.8.6	Suitable and sufficient hand-washing facilities shall be provided at access to, and at other appropriate points within, production areas. Such hand-wash facilities shall provide as a minimum: ● sufficient quantity of water at a suitable temperature ● liquid soap ● single use towels or suitably designed and located air driers ● water taps with hand-free operation ● advisory signs to prompt hand-washing.
4.8.7	Toilets shall be adequately segregated and shall not open directly into production, packing and storage areas. Toilets shall be provided with hand-washing facilities comprising: ● basins with soap and water at a suitable temperature ● adequate hand-drying facilities ● advisory signs to prompt hand-washing. Where hand-washing facilities within toilet facilities are the only facilities provided before re-entering production, the requirements of 4.8.6 shall apply and signs shall be in place to direct people to hand-wash facilities before entering production.

Clause	Requirements
4.8.8	Where smoking is allowed under national law, designated controlled smoking areas shall be provided which are both isolated from production areas to an extent that ensures smoke cannot reach the product and fitted with sufficient extraction to the exterior of the building. Adequate arrangements for dealing with smokers' waste shall be provided at smoking facilities, both inside and at exterior locations.
4.8.9	All food brought into manufacturing premises by staff shall be appropriately stored in a clean and hygienic state. No food shall be taken into storage, processing or production areas. Where eating of food is allowed outside during breaks, this shall be in suitable designated areas with appropriate control of waste.
4.8.10	Where catering facilities are provided on the premises, they shall be suitably controlled to prevent contamination of product (e.g. as a source of food poisoning or introduction of allergenic material to the site).

4.9   Chemical and physical product contamination control

Raw material handling, preparation, processing, packing and storage areas

Appropriate facilities and procedures shall be in place to control the risk of chemical or physical contamination of product.

4.9.1   Chemical control

Clause	Requirements
4.9.1.1	Processes shall be in place to manage the use, storage and handling of non-food chemicals to prevent chemical contamination. These shall include as a minimum: ● an approved list of chemicals for purchase ● availability of material safety data sheets and specifications ● confirmation of suitability for use in a food processing environment ● avoidance of strongly scented products ● the labelling and/or identification of containers of chemicals at all times ● segregated and secure storage with restricted access to authorised personnel ● use by trained personnel only.
4.9.1.2	Where strongly scented or taint-forming materials have to be used, for instance for building work, procedures shall be in place to prevent the risk of taint contamination of products.

4.9.2   Metal control

Clause	Requirements
4.9.2.1	There shall be a documented policy for the control of the use of sharp metal implements including knives, cutting blades on equipment, needles and wires. This shall include a record of inspection for damage and the investigation of any lost items. Snap-off blade knives shall not be used.
4.9.2.2	The purchase of ingredients and packaging which use staples or other foreign-body hazards as part of the packaging materials shall be avoided. Staples and paper clips shall not be used in open product areas. Where staples or other items are present as packaging materials or closures, appropriate precautions shall be taken to minimise the risk of product contamination.

4.9.3   Glass, brittle plastic, ceramics and similar materials

Clause	Requirements
4.9.3.1	Glass or other brittle materials shall be excluded or protected against breakage in areas where open products are handled or there is a risk of product contamination.
4.9.3.2	Documented procedures for handling glass and other brittle materials shall be in place and implemented to ensure that necessary precautions are taken. Procedures shall include as a minimum: • a list of items detailing location, number, type and condition • recorded checks of condition of items, carried out at a specified frequency that is based on the level of risk to the product • details on cleaning or replacing items to minimise potential for product contamination.
4.9.3.3	Documented procedures detailing the action to be taken in case of breakage of glass or other brittle items shall be implemented and include the following: • quarantining the products and production area that were potentially affected • cleaning the production area • inspecting the production area and authorising to continue production • changing of workwear and inspection of footwear • specifying those staff authorised to carry out the above points • recording the breakage incident.

4.9.3.4 Products packed into glass or other brittle containers

Clause	Requirements
4.9.3.4.1	The storage of the containers shall be segregated from the storage of raw materials, product or other packaging.
4.9.3.4.2	Systems shall be in place to manage container breakages between the container cleaning/ inspection point and container closure. This shall include, as a minimum, documented instructions which ensure: ● the removal and disposal of at-risk products in the vicinity of the breakage; this may be specific for different equipment or areas of the production line. ● the effective cleaning of the line or equipment which may be contaminated by fragments of the container. Cleaning shall not result in the further dispersal of fragments, for instance by the use of high pressure water or air. ● the use of dedicated, clearly identifiable cleaning equipment (e.g. colour coded) for removal of container breakages. Such equipment shall be stored separately from other cleaning equipment. ● the use of dedicated, accessible lidded waste containers for the collection of damaged containers and fragments. ● a documented inspection of production equipment is undertaken following the cleaning of a breakage to ensure cleaning has effectively removed any risk of further contamination. ● authorisation is given for production to re-start following cleaning. ● the area around the line is kept clear of broken glass.
4.9.3.4.3	Records shall be maintained of all container breakages on the line. Where no breakages have occurred during a production period, this shall also be recorded. This record shall be reviewed to identify trends and potential line or container improvements.

4.9.4   Wood

Clause	Requirements
4.9.4.1	Wood should not be used in open product areas except where this is a process requirement (e.g. maturation of products in wood). Where the use of wood cannot be avoided, the condition of wood shall be continually monitored to ensure it is in good condition and free from damage or splinters which could contaminate products.

4.10 Foreign body detection and removal equipment

The risk of product contamination shall be reduced or eliminated by the effective use of equipment to remove or detect foreign bodies.

4.10.1 Foreign body detection and removal equipment

Clause	Requirements
4.10.1.1	A documented assessment in association with the HACCP study shall be carried out on each production process to identify the potential use of equipment to detect or remove foreign body contamination. Typical equipment to be considered may include: ● filters ● sieves ● metal detection ● magnets ● optical sorting equipment ● X-ray detection equipment ● other physical separation equipment e.g. gravity separation, fluid bed technology.
4.10.1.2	The type, location and sensitivity of the detection and/or removal method shall be specified as part of the company's documented system. Industry best practice shall be applied with regard to the nature of the ingredient, material, product and/or the packed product. The location of the equipment or any other factors influencing the sensitivity of the equipment shall be validated and justified.
4.10.1.3	The company shall ensure that the frequency of the testing of the foreign body detection and/or removal equipment is defined and takes into consideration: ● specific customer requirements ● the company's ability to identify, hold and prevent the release of any affected materials, should the equipment fail.
4.10.1.4	Where foreign material is detected or removed by the equipment, the source of any unexpected material shall be investigated. Information on rejected materials shall be used to identify trends and where possible instigate preventive action to reduce the occurrence of contamination by the foreign material.

4.10.2 Filters and sieves

Clause	Requirements
4.10.2.1	Filters and sieves used for foreign body control shall be of a specified mesh size or gauge and designed to provide the maximum practical protection for the product. Material retained or removed by the system shall be examined and recorded to identify contamination risks.
4.10.2.2	Filters and sieves shall be regularly inspected or tested for damage on a documented frequency based on risk. Records shall be maintained of the checks. Where defective filters or sieves are identified this shall be recorded and the potential for contamination of products investigated and appropriate action taken.

4.10.3 Metal detectors and X-ray equipment

Clause	Requirements
4.10.3.1	Metal detection equipment shall be in place unless risk assessment demonstrates that this does not improve the protection of final products from metal contamination. Where metal detectors are not used justification shall be documented. The absence of metal detection would only normally be based on the use of an alternative, more effective, method of protection (e.g. use of X-ray, fine sieves or filtration of products).
4.10.3.2	Where metal detectors or X-ray equipment is used, this shall be situated at the latest practical step in the process flow and, wherever possible, after the product has been packaged.
4.10.3.3	The metal detector or X-ray equipment shall incorporate one of the following: ● an automatic rejection device, for continuous in-line systems, which shall either divert contaminated product out of the product flow or to a secure unit accessible only to authorised personnel ● a belt stop system with an alarm where the product cannot be automatically rejected, e.g. for very large packs ● in-line detectors which identify the location of the contaminant shall be operated to allow effective segregation of the affected product.
4.10.3.4	The company shall establish and implement documented procedures for the operation and testing of the metal or X-ray equipment. This shall include as a minimum: ● responsibilities for the testing of equipment ● the operating effectiveness and sensitivity of the equipment and any variation to this for particular products ● the methods and frequency of checking the detector ● recording of the results of checks.
4.10.3.5	Metal detector checking procedures shall be based on best practice and shall as a minimum include: ● use of test pieces incorporating a sphere of metal of a known diameter. The test pieces shall be marked with the size and type of test material contained. ● tests carried out using separate test pieces containing ferrous metal, stainless steel and typically non-ferrous metal, unless the product is within a foil container. ● a test that both the detection and rejection mechanisms are working effectively under normal working conditions. ● checks that test the memory/reset function of the metal detector by passing successive test packs through the unit. In addition, where metal detectors are incorporated on conveyors: ● the test piece shall be passed as close as possible to the centre of the metal detector aperture and wherever possible be carried out by inserting the test piece within a clearly identified sample pack of the food being produced at the time of the test. Where in-line metal detectors are used the test piece shall be placed in the product flow wherever this is possible.
4.10.3.6	The company shall establish and implement corrective action and reporting procedures in the event of the testing procedure identifying any failure of the foreign body detector. Action shall include a combination of isolation, quarantining and re-inspection of all product produced since the last successful test.

4.10.4 Magnets

Clause	Requirements
4.10.4.1	The type, location and the strength of magnets shall be fully documented. Documented procedures shall be in place for the inspection, cleaning, strength testing and integrity checks. Records of all checks shall be maintained.

4.10.5 Optical sorting equipment

Clause	Requirements
4.10.5.1	Each unit shall be checked in accordance with the manufacturer's instructions or recommendations. Checks shall be documented.

4.10.6 Container cleanliness – glass jars, cans and other rigid containers

Clause	Requirements
4.10.6.1	Based on risk assessment, procedures shall be implemented to minimise foreign body contamination originating with the packaging container (e.g. jars, cans and other preformed rigid containers). This may include the use of covered conveyors, container inversion and foreign body removal through rinsing with water or air jets.
4.10.6.2	The effectiveness of the container cleaning equipment shall be checked and recorded during each production. Where the system incorporates a rejection system for dirty or damaged containers, the check shall incorporate a test of both the detection and effective rejection of the test container.

4.11   Housekeeping and hygiene

FUNDAMENTAL

Housekeeping and cleaning systems shall be in place which ensure appropriate standards of hygiene are maintained at all times and the risk of product contamination is minimised.

Clause	Requirements
4.11.1	Documented cleaning procedures shall be in place and maintained for the building, plant and all equipment. Cleaning procedures shall as a minimum include the: ● responsibility for cleaning ● item/area to be cleaned ● frequency of cleaning ● method of cleaning, including dismantling equipment for cleaning purposes where required ● cleaning chemicals and concentrations ● cleaning materials to be used ● cleaning records and responsibility for verification. The frequency and methods of cleaning shall be based on risk. The procedures shall be implemented to ensure appropriate standards of cleaning are achieved.
4.11.2	Limits of acceptable and unacceptable cleaning performance shall be defined, based on the potential hazards (e.g. microbiological, allergen or foreign body contamination). Acceptable levels of cleaning may be defined by visual appearance, ATP bioluminescence techniques (see Glossary), microbiological testing or chemical testing as appropriate. The cleaning and disinfection procedures and frequency shall be validated and records maintained.
4.11.3	The resources for undertaking cleaning shall be available. Where it is necessary to dismantle equipment for cleaning purposes or to enter large equipment for cleaning, this shall be appropriately scheduled and, where necessary, planned for non-production periods. Cleaning staff shall be adequately trained or engineering support provided where access within equipment is required for cleaning.
4.11.4	The cleanliness of equipment shall be checked before equipment is released back into full production. The results of checks on cleaning, including visual, analytical and microbiological checks, shall be recorded and used to identify trends in cleaning performance and instigate improvements where required.
4.11.5	Cleaning equipment shall be: ● fit for purpose ● suitably identified for intended use, e.g. colour coded or labelled ● cleaned and stored in a hygienic manner to prevent contamination. Equipment used for cleaning in **high-care and high-risk** areas shall be dedicated for use in that area.

4.11.6   Cleaning in place (CIP)

Clause	Requirements
4.11.6.1	Cleaning-in-place (CIP) facilities, where used, shall be monitored and maintained to ensure their effective operation.
4.11.6.2	A schematic plan of the layout of the CIP system shall be available. There shall be an inspection report or other verification that:
	• systems are hygienically designed with no dead areas, limited interruptions to flow streams and good system drain ability.
	• scavenge pumps are operated to ensure that there is no build-up of cleaning fluids in the vessels.
	• spray balls effectively clean vessels by providing full surface coverage and are periodically inspected for blockages. Rotating spray devices should have a defined operational time.
	• CIP equipment has adequate separation from active product lines, e.g. through the use of double seat valves, manually controlled links or blanks in pipework.
	The system shall be revalidated following alterations or additions to the CIP equipment. A log of changes to the CIP system shall be maintained.
4.11.6.3	The CIP equipment shall be operated to ensure effective cleaning is carried out:
	• The process parameters, time, detergent concentrations, flow rate and temperatures shall be defined to ensure removal of the appropriate target hazard, e.g. soil, allergens, vegetative microorganisms, spores. This shall be validated and records of the validation maintained.
	• Detergent concentrations shall be checked routinely.
	• Process verification shall be undertaken by analysis of rinse waters and/or first product through the line for the presence of cleaning fluids or by tests of ATP (bioluminescence techniques) allergens or micro-organisms as appropriate.
	• Detergent tanks shall be kept stocked up and a log maintained of when these are filled and emptied. Recovered pre-rinse solutions shall be monitored for a build-up of carry-over from the detergent tanks.
	• Filters, where fitted, shall be cleaned and inspected at a defined frequency.

4.12   Waste/waste disposal

Waste disposal shall be managed in accordance with legal requirements and to prevent accumulation, risk of contamination and the attraction of pests.

Clause	Requirements
4.12.1	Where licensing is required for the disposal of categorised waste, it shall be removed by licensed contractors and records of disposal shall be maintained and available for audit.
4.12.2	Food products intended to be supplied for animal feed shall be segregated from waste and managed in accordance with relevant legislative requirements.
4.12.3	External waste collection containers and rooms housing waste facilities shall be managed to minimise risk. These shall be: ● clearly identified ● designed for ease of use and effective cleaning ● well-maintained to allow cleaning and, where required, disinfection ● emptied at appropriate frequencies ● covered or doors kept closed as appropriate.
4.12.4	If unsafe products or substandard trademarked materials are transferred to a third party for destruction or disposal, that third party shall be a specialist in secure product or waste disposal and shall provide records which includes the quantity of waste collected for destruction or disposal.

4.13   Pest control

The whole site shall have an effective preventive pest control programme in place to minimise the risk of infestation and there shall be the resources available to rapidly respond to any issues which occur to prevent risk to products.

Clause	Requirements
4.13.1	The company shall either contract the services of a competent pest control organisation, or shall have appropriately trained staff, for the regular inspection and treatment of the site to deter and eradicate infestation. The frequency of inspections shall be determined by risk assessment and shall be documented. Where the services of a pest control contractor are employed, the service contract shall be clearly defined and reflect the activities of the site.
4.13.2	Where a company undertakes its own pest control, it shall be able to effectively demonstrate that: ● pest control operations are undertaken by trained and competent staff with sufficient knowledge to select appropriate pest control chemicals and proofing methods and understand the limitations of use, relevant to the biology of the pests associated with the site ● sufficient resources are available to respond to any infestation issues ● there is ready access to specialist technical knowledge when required ● legislation governing the use of pest control products is understood ● dedicated locked facilities are used for the storage of pesticides.

Clause	Requirements
4.13.3	Pest control documentation and records shall be maintained. This shall include as a minimum: ● an up-to-date plan of the full site identifying numbered pest control device locations ● identification of the baits and/or monitoring devices on site ● clearly defined responsibilities for site management and for the contractor ● details of pest control products used, including instructions for their effective use and action to be taken in case of emergencies ● any observed pest activity ● details of pest control treatments undertaken.
4.13.4	Bait stations shall be robust, of tamper resistant construction, secured in place and appropriately located to prevent contamination risk to product. Missing bait boxes shall be recorded, reviewed and investigated. Toxic rodent baits shall not be used within production areas or storage areas where open product is present except when treating an active infestation.
4.13.5	Fly-killing devices and/or pheromone traps shall be correctly sited and operational. If there is a danger of insects being expelled from a fly-killing extermination device and contaminating the product, alternative systems and equipment shall be used.
4.13.6	In the event of infestation, or evidence of pest activity, immediate action shall be taken to eliminate the hazard. Any potentially affected products should be subject to the non-conforming product procedure.
4.13.7	Records of pest control inspections, pest proofing and hygiene recommendations and actions taken shall be maintained. It shall be the responsibility of the company to ensure all of the relevant recommendations made by their contractor or in-house expert are carried out in a timely manner.
4.13.8	An in-depth, documented pest control survey shall be undertaken at a frequency based on risk, but typically quarterly, by a pest control expert to review the pest control measures in place. The timing of the survey shall be such as to allow access to equipment for inspection where a risk of stored product insect infestation exists.
4.13.9	Results of pest control inspections shall be assessed and analysed for trends on a regular basis, but as a minimum: ● in the event of an infestation ● annually. This shall include a catch analysis from trapping devices to identify problem areas. The analysis shall be used as a basis for improving the pest control procedures.

4.14   Storage facilities

All facilities used for the storage of ingredients, in-process product and finished products shall be suitable for its purpose.

Clause	Requirements
4.14.1	Documented procedures to maintain product safety and quality during storage shall be developed on the basis of risk assessment, understood by relevant staff and implemented accordingly. These may include as appropriate: ● managing chilled and frozen product transfer between temperature controlled areas ● segregation of products where necessary to avoid cross-contamination (physical, microbiological or allergens) or taint uptake ● storing materials off the floor and away from walls ● specific handling or stacking requirements to prevent product damage.
4.14.2	Where temperature control is required, the storage area shall be capable of maintaining product temperature within specification and operated to ensure specified temperatures are maintained. Temperature recording equipment with suitable temperature alarms shall be fitted to all storage facilities **or** there shall be a system of recorded manual temperature checks, typically on at least a four-hourly basis or at a frequency which allows for intervention before product temperatures exceed defined limits for the safety, legality or quality of products.
4.14.3	Where controlled atmosphere storage is required, the storage conditions shall be specified and effectively controlled. Records shall be maintained of the storage conditions.
4.14.4	Where storage outside is necessary, items shall be protected from contamination and deterioration.
4.14.5	Receipt documents and/or product identification shall facilitate correct stock rotation of raw materials, intermediate products and finished products in storage and ensure materials are used in the correct order in relation to their manufacturing date and within the prescribed shelf life.

4.15   Dispatch and transport

Procedures shall be in place to ensure that the management of dispatch and of the vehicles and containers used for transporting products from the site do not present a risk to the safety or quality of the products.

Clause	Requirements
4.15.1	Documented procedures to maintain product safety and quality during loading and transportation shall be developed and implemented. These may include as appropriate: ● controlling temperature of loading dock areas ● the use of covered bays for vehicle loading or unloading ● securing loads on pallets to prevent movement during transit ● inspection of loads prior to dispatch.
4.15.2	Traceability shall be ensured during transportation. There shall be a clear record of dispatch and receipt of goods and materials demonstrating that sufficient checks have been completed during the transfer of goods.
4.15.3	All vehicles or containers used for the dispatch of products shall be inspected prior to loading to ensure that they are fit for purpose. This shall ensure that they are: ● in a suitably clean condition ● free from strong odours which may cause taint to products ● suitably maintained to prevent damage to products during transit ● equipped to ensure any temperature requirements can be maintained. Records of inspections shall be maintained.
4.15.4	Where temperature control is required, the transport shall be capable of maintaining product temperature within specification, under minimum and maximum load. Temperature data-logging devices which can be interrogated to confirm time/temperature conditions **or** a system to verify and record at predetermined frequencies the correct operation of refrigeration equipment shall be used and records maintained.
4.15.5	Maintenance systems and documented cleaning procedures shall be maintained for all vehicles and equipment used for loading/unloading (e.g. hoses connecting to silo installations). There shall be records of the measures taken.
4.15.6	The company shall have documented procedures for the transport of products, which shall include: ● any restrictions on the use of mixed loads ● requirements for the security of products during transit, particularly when vehicles are parked and unattended ● clear instructions in the case of vehicle breakdown, accident or failure of refrigeration systems which ensure the safety of the products is assessed and records maintained.
4.15.7	Where the company employs third-party contractors, all the requirements specified in this section shall be clearly defined in the contract and verified or the contracted company shall be certificated to the *Global Standard for Storage and Distribution* or similar internationally recognised Standard.

5   Product Control

5.1   Product design/development

Product design and development procedures shall be in place for new products or processes and any changes to product, packaging or manufacturing processes to ensure that safe and legal products are produced.

Clause	Requirements
5.1.1	The company shall provide clear guidelines on any restrictions to the scope of new product developments to control the introduction of hazards which would be unacceptable to the company or customers (e.g. the introduction of allergens, glass packaging or microbiological risks).
5.1.2	All new products and changes to product formulation, packaging or methods of processing shall be formally approved by the HACCP team leader or authorised HACCP committee member. This shall ensure that hazards have been assessed and suitable controls, identified through the HACCP system, are implemented. This approval shall be granted before products are introduced into the factory environment.
5.1.3	Trials using production equipment shall be carried out where it is necessary to validate that product formulation and manufacturing processes are capable of producing a safe product of the required quality.
5.1.4	Shelf-life trials shall be undertaken using documented protocols reflecting conditions experienced during storage and handling. Results shall be recorded and retained and shall confirm compliance with relevant microbiological, chemical and organoleptic criteria. Where shelf-life trials prior to production are impractical, for instance for some long-life products, a documented science-based justification for the assigned shelf life shall be produced.
5.1.5	All products shall be labelled to meet legal requirements for the designated country of use and shall include information to allow the safe handling, display, storage, preparation and use of the product within the food supply chain or by the customer. There shall be a process to verify that ingredient and allergen labelling is correct based on the product recipe.
5.1.6	Where a product is designed to enable a claim to be made to satisfy a consumer group (e.g. a nutritional claim, reduced sugar), the company shall ensure that the product formulation and production process is fully validated to meet the stated claim.

5.2   Management of allergens

FUNDAMENTAL

The company shall have a developed system for the management of allergenic materials which minimises the risk of allergen contamination of products and meets legal requirements for labelling.

Clause	Requirements
5.2.1	The company shall carry out an assessment of raw materials to establish the presence and likelihood of contamination by **allergens** (refer to glossary). This shall include review of raw material specifications and, where required, obtain additional information from suppliers, for example through questionnaires to understand the allergen status of the raw material, its ingredients and the factory in which it is produced.
5.2.2	The company shall identify and list allergen-containing materials handled on site. This shall include raw materials, processing aids, intermediate and finished products and any new product development ingredients or products.
5.2.3	A documented risk assessment shall be carried out to identify routes of contamination and establish documented policies and procedures for handling raw materials, intermediate and finished products to ensure cross-contamination is avoided. This shall include: ● consideration of the physical state of the allergenic material, i.e. powder, liquid, particulate ● identification of potential points of cross-contamination through the process flow ● assessment of the risk of allergen cross-contamination at each process step ● identification of suitable controls to reduce or eliminate the risk of cross-contamination.
5.2.4	Documented procedures shall be established to ensure the effective management of allergenic materials to prevent cross-contamination into products not containing the allergen. This shall include as appropriate: ● physical or time segregation whilst allergen-containing materials are being stored, processed or packed ● the use of separate or additional protective over clothing when handling allergenic materials ● use of identified, dedicated equipment and utensils for processing ● scheduling of production to reduce changes between products containing an allergen and products not containing the allergen ● systems to restrict the movement of airborne dust containing allergenic material ● waste handling and spillage controls ● restrictions on food brought onto site by staff, visitors, contractors and for catering purposes.
5.2.5	Where rework is used, or reworking operations carried out, procedures shall be implemented to ensure rework containing allergens is not used in products that do not already contain the allergen.
5.2.6	Where the nature of the production process is such that cross-contamination from an allergen cannot be prevented, a warning shall be included on the label. National guidelines or codes of practice shall be used when making such a warning statement.
5.2.7	Where a claim is made regarding the suitability of a food for allergy or food sensitivity sufferers, the company shall ensure that the production process is fully validated to meet the stated claim. This shall be documented.

Clause	Requirements
5.2.8	Equipment or area cleaning procedures shall be designed to remove or reduce to acceptable levels any potential cross-contamination by allergens. The cleaning methods shall be validated to ensure they are effective and the effectiveness of the procedure routinely verified. Cleaning equipment used to clean allergenic materials shall either be identifiable and specific for allergen use, single use, or effectively cleaned after use.
5.2.9	All relevant personnel, including engineers, temporary staff and contractors, shall have received general allergen awareness training and be trained in the company's allergen-handling procedures.
5.2.10	An effective system of documented checks shall be in place at line start-up, following product changeover and changes in batches of packaging to ensure that the labels applied are correct for the products packed.

5.3　Provenance, assured status and claims of identity preserved materials

Systems of traceability, identification and segregation of raw materials, intermediate and finished products shall be in place to ensure that all claims relating to provenance or assured status can be substantiated.

Clause	Requirements
5.3.1	Where claims are to be made on finished packs about the provenance, assured or 'identity preserved' status (see Glossary) of raw materials used, the status of each batch of the raw material shall be verified and records maintained.
5.3.2	Where a claim is made relating to the provenance, assured or identity preserved status of a product or ingredient, the facility shall maintain purchasing records, traceability of raw material usage and final product packing records to substantiate claims. The company shall undertake documented mass balance tests at least every six months and at a frequency to meet the particular scheme requirements.
5.3.3	The process flow for the production of products where claims are made shall be documented and potential areas for contamination or loss of identity identified. Appropriate controls shall be established to ensure the integrity of the product claims.

5.4 Product packaging

Product packaging shall be appropriate for the intended use and shall be stored under conditions to minimise contamination and deterioration.

Clause	Requirements
5.4.1	When purchasing or specifying food contact packaging the supplier of packaging materials shall be made aware of any particular characteristics of the food (e.g. high fat content, pH or usage conditions such as microwaving) which may affect packaging suitability. Certificates of conformity or other evidence shall be available for product packaging to confirm it conforms to relevant food safety legislation and is suitable for its intended use.
5.4.2	Where appropriate, packaging shall be stored away from raw materials and finished product. Any part-used packaging materials suitable for use shall be effectively protected from contamination and clearly identified before being returned to an appropriate storage area. Obsolete packaging shall be stored in a separate area and systems shall be in place to prevent accidental use.
5.4.3	Product contact liners (or raw material/work-in-progress contact liners) purchased by the company shall be appropriately coloured and resistant to tearing to prevent accidental contamination.

5.5 Product inspection and laboratory testing

The company shall undertake or subcontract inspection and analyses which are critical to confirm product safety, legality and quality, using appropriate procedures, facilities and standards.

5.5.1 Product inspection and testing

Clause	Requirements
5.5.1.1	There shall be a scheduled programme of testing covering products and the processing environment which may include microbiological, chemical, physical and organoleptic testing according to risk. The methods, frequency and specified limits shall be documented.
5.5.1.2	Test and inspection results shall be recorded and reviewed regularly to identify trends. Appropriate actions shall be implemented promptly to address any unsatisfactory results or trends.
5.5.1.3	The company shall ensure that a system of on-going shelf-life assessment is in place. This shall be based on risk and shall include microbiological and sensory analysis as well as relevant chemical factors such as pH and a_w. Records and results from shelf life tests shall validate the shelf life period indicated on the product.

5.5.2   Laboratory testing

Clause	Requirements
5.5.2.1	Pathogen testing shall be subcontracted to an external laboratory or, where conducted internally, the laboratory facility shall be fully segregated from the manufacturing site and have operating procedures to prevent any risk of product contamination.
5.5.2.2	Where routine testing laboratories are present on a manufacturing site, they shall be located, designed and operated to eliminate potential risks to product safety. Controls shall be documented, implemented and shall include consideration of the following: ● design and operation of drainage and ventilation systems ● access and security of the facility ● movement of laboratory personnel ● protective clothing arrangements ● processes for obtaining product samples ● disposal of laboratory waste.
5.5.2.3	Where the company undertakes or subcontracts analyses which are critical to product safety or legality, the laboratory or subcontractors shall have gained recognised laboratory accreditation or operate in accordance with the requirements and principles of ISO 17025. Documented justification shall be available where accredited methods are not undertaken.
5.5.2.4	Procedures shall be in place to ensure reliability of laboratory results, other than those critical to safety and legality specified in 5.5.2.3. These shall include: ● use of recognised test methods, where available ● documented testing procedures ● ensuring staff are suitably qualified and/or trained and competent to carry out the analysis required ● use of a system to verify the accuracy of test results, e.g. ring or proficiency testing ● use of appropriately calibrated and maintained equipment.

5.6   Product release

The company shall ensure that finished product is not released unless all agreed procedures have been followed.

Clause	Requirements
5.6.1	Where products require positive release, procedures shall be in place to ensure that release does not occur until all release criteria have been completed and release authorised.

6 Process Control

6.1 Control of operations

FUNDAMENTAL

The company shall operate to documented procedures and/or work instructions that ensure the production of consistently safe and legal product with the desired quality characteristics, in full compliance with the HACCP food safety plan.

Clause	Requirements
6.1.1	Documented process specifications and work instructions shall be available for the key processes in the production of products to ensure product safety, legality and quality. The specifications as appropriate shall include: ● recipes – including identification of any allergens ● mixing instructions, speed, time ● equipment process settings ● cooking times and temperatures ● cooling times and temperatures ● labelling instructions ● coding and shelf life marking ● any additional critical control points identified in the HACCP plan.
6.1.2	Process monitoring, such as of temperature, time, pressure and chemical properties, shall be implemented, adequately controlled and recorded to ensure that product is produced within the required process specification.
6.1.3	In circumstances where process parameters are controlled by in-line monitoring devices, these shall be linked to a suitable failure alert system that is routinely tested.
6.1.4	Where variation in processing conditions may occur within equipment critical to the safety or quality of products, the processing characteristics shall be validated at a frequency based on risk and performance of equipment (e.g. heat distribution in retorts, ovens and processing vessels; temperature distribution in freezers and cold stores).
6.1.5	In the case of equipment failure or deviation of the process from specification, procedures shall be in place to establish the safety status and quality of the product to determine the action to be taken.
6.1.6	Documented checks of the production line shall be carried out before commencing production and following changes of product. These shall ensure that lines have been suitably cleaned and are ready for production. Documented checks shall be carried out at product changes to ensure all products and packaging from the previous production have been removed from the line before changing to the next production.
6.1.7	Documented procedures shall be in place to ensure that products are packed into the correct packaging and correctly labelled. These shall include checks at the start of packing, during the packaging run, following packaging changes and when changing batches of packaging materials, in order to ensure that correct packaging materials are used. The procedures shall also include verification of any code information or other printing carried out at the packing stage.

6.2   Quantity – weight, volume and number control

The company shall operate a quantity control system which conforms to legal requirements in the country where the product is sold and any additional industry sector codes or specified customer requirement.

Clause	Requirements
6.2.1	The frequency and methodology of quantity checking shall meet the requirements of appropriate legislation governing quantity verification, and records of checks shall be maintained.
6.2.2	Where the quantity of the product is not governed by legislative requirements (e.g. bulk quantity), the product must conform to customer requirements and records shall be maintained.

6.3   Calibration and control of measuring and monitoring devices

The company shall be able to demonstrate that measuring and monitoring equipment is sufficiently accurate and reliable to provide confidence in measurement results.

Clause	Requirements
6.3.1	The company shall identify and control measuring equipment used to monitor CCPs, product safety and legality. This shall include as a minimum: ● a documented list of equipment and its location ● an identification code and calibration due date ● prevention from adjustment by unauthorised staff ● protection from damage, deterioration or misuse.
6.3.2	All identified measuring devices, including new equipment, shall be checked and where necessary adjusted: ● at a predetermined frequency, based on risk assessment ● to a defined method traceable to a recognised national or international Standard where possible. Results shall be documented. Equipment shall be readable and be of a suitable accuracy for the measurements it is required to perform.
6.3.3	Reference measuring equipment shall be calibrated and traceable to a recognised national or international Standard and records maintained.
6.3.4	Procedures shall be in place to record actions to be taken when the prescribed measuring and monitoring devices are found not to be operating within specified limits. Where the safety or legality of products is based on equipment found to be inaccurate, action shall to be taken to ensure at-risk product is not offered for sale.

Personnel

7.1 Training

Raw material handling, preparation, processing, packing and storage areas

FUNDAMENTAL

 The company shall ensure that all personnel performing work that affects product safety, legality and quality are demonstrably competent to carry out their activity, through training, work experience or qualification.

Clause	Requirements
7.1.1	All relevant personnel, including temporary staff and contractors, shall be appropriately trained prior to commencing work and adequately supervised throughout the working period.
7.1.2	Where personnel are engaged in activities relating to critical control points, relevant training and competency assessment shall be in place.
7.1.3	The company shall put in place documented programmes covering the training needs of relevant personnel. These shall include as a minimum: ● identifying the necessary competencies for specific roles ● providing training or other action to ensure staff have the necessary competencies ● reviewing the effectiveness of training ● the delivery of training in the appropriate language of trainees.
7.1.4	Records of all training shall be available. This shall include as a minimum: ● the name of the trainee and confirmation of attendance ● the date and duration of the training ● the title or course contents, as appropriate ● the training provider. Where training is undertaken by agencies on behalf of the company, records of the training shall be available.
7.1.5	The company shall routinely review the competencies of its staff. As appropriate, it shall provide relevant training. This may be in the form of training, refresher training, coaching, mentoring or on-the-job experience.

7.2   Personal hygiene

Raw materials handling, preparation, processing, packing and storage areas

The company's personal hygiene standards shall be appropriate to the products produced, documented, and adopted by all personnel, including agency staff, contractors and visitors to the production facility.

Clause	Requirements
7.2.1	The requirements for personal hygiene shall be documented and communicated to all personnel. This shall include as a minimum the following requirements: ● Watches shall not be worn. ● Jewellery shall not be worn, with the exception of a plain wedding ring or wedding wristband. ● Rings and studs in exposed parts of the body, such as ears, noses, tongues and eyebrows, shall not be worn. ● Fingernails shall be kept short, clean and unvarnished. False fingernails shall not be permitted. ● Excessive perfume or aftershave shall not be worn. Compliance with the requirements shall be checked routinely.
7.2.2	Hand cleaning shall be performed on entry to the production areas and at a frequency that is appropriate to minimise the risk of product contamination.
7.2.3	All cuts and grazes on exposed skin shall be covered by an appropriately coloured plaster that is different from the product colour (preferably blue) and containing a metal detectable strip. These shall be company issued and monitored. Where appropriate, in addition to the plaster, a glove shall be worn.
7.2.4	Where metal detection equipment is used, a sample from each batch of plasters shall be successfully tested through the equipment and records shall be kept.
7.2.5	Processes and written instructions for staff shall be in place to control the use and storage of personal medicines, so as to minimise the risk of product contamination.

7.3   Medical screening

The company shall ensure that procedures are in place to ensure that employees, agency staff, contractors or visitors are not a source of transmission of food-borne diseases to products.

Clause	Requirements
7.3.1	The company shall have a procedure which enables notification by employees, including temporary employees, of any relevant infection, disease or condition with which they may have been in contact or be suffering from.
7.3.2	Where there may be a risk to product safety, visitors and contractors shall be required to complete a health questionnaire or otherwise confirm that they are not suffering from a condition which may put product safety at risk, prior to entering the raw material, preparation, processing, packing and storage areas.
7.3.3	There shall be documented procedures for employees, contractors and visitors, relating to action to be taken where they may be suffering from or have been in contact with an infectious disease. Expert medical advice shall be sought where required.

7.4   Protective clothing

Employees or visitors to production areas

Suitable company-issued protective clothing shall be worn by employees, contractors or visitors working in or entering production areas.

Clause	Requirements
7.4.1	The company shall document and communicate to all employees, contractors or visitors the rules regarding the wearing of protective clothing in specified work areas (e.g. **high-care** or low-risk areas). This shall also include policies relating to the wearing of protective clothing away from the production environment (e.g. removal before entering toilets, use of canteen and smoking areas).
7.4.2	Protective clothing shall be available that: ● is provided in sufficient numbers for each employee ● is of suitable design to prevent contamination of the product (as a minimum containing no external pockets above the waist or sewn on buttons) ● fully contains all scalp hair to prevent product contamination ● includes snoods for beards and moustaches where required to prevent product contamination.
7.4.3	Laundering of protective clothing shall take place by an approved contracted or in-house laundry using defined and verified criteria to validate the effectiveness of the laundering process. Washing of workwear by the employee is exceptional but shall be acceptable where the protective clothing is to protect the employee from the products handled and the clothing is worn in enclosed product or low-risk areas only.
7.4.4	Where protective clothing for **high-care or high-risk areas** is provided by a contracted laundry, this shall be audited either directly or by a third party, or should have a relevant certification. The laundry must operate procedures which ensure: ● effective cleaning of the protective clothing ● clothes are commercially sterile following the washing and drying process ● adequate segregation between dirty and cleaned clothes ● cleaned clothes are protected from contamination until delivered to the site, e.g. by the use of covers or bags.
7.4.5	If gloves are used, they shall be replaced regularly. Where appropriate, gloves shall be suitable for food use, of a disposable type, of a distinctive colour (blue where possible), be intact and not shed loose fibres.
7.4.6	Where items of personal protective clothing that are not suitable for laundering are provided (such as chain mail, gloves and aprons), these shall be cleaned and sanitised at a frequency based on risk.

SECTION III

THE AUDIT PROTOCOL

Section III

The Audit Protocol

Part 1 – General Audit Protocol

1 Introduction

The *Global Standard for Food Safety* provides companies with a series of options with which to be audited and certificated. This flexible approach is in response to market demand and allows companies to choose an audit option which best suits their customers' requirements, factory operations and the maturity of their food safety systems.

The general audit protocol describes the requirements for auditing and certification which is applicable to all of the audit programmes and should be read and fully understood. The process is summarised in Figure 1.

Each of the audit options has its own particular characteristics and these are described in detail in Part 2 of this section (refer to page 76).

Every effort has been made to ensure that the content of this audit protocol is accurate at the time of printing. However, it may be subject to minor change, and reference should be made to the BRC Global Standards website www.brcglobalstandards.com, where changes will be published.

Conformance by the company to the requirements of the *Global Standard for Food Safety* and its suitability for the awarding and continuing retention of certification will be assessed by an independent audit company – the Certification Body. Certification will be graded according to the audit option selected and the number and type of non-conformities, which shall also influence the frequency of ongoing audits. This section describes the process to be followed by a company seeking certification.

2 Self-assessment of Compliance with the Standard

It is essential that the company is assessed against the current issue of the *Global Standard for Food Safety* and that this is available throughout the certification process. The Standard has been translated into a number of different languages and these are available either as a downloadable pdf or hard copy from www.brcbookshop.com.

The Standard should be read and understood and a preliminary self-assessment should be conducted by the company against the Standard to prepare for the audit. Any areas of non-conformity should be addressed by the company. Further information and guidance to ensure compliance with the Standard, including training courses and guideline booklets, are available from the BRC Global Standards website.

An optional on-site pre-assessment may be carried out by the selected Certification Body in preparation for the audit, to provide guidance to the company on the process of certification. It should be noted, however, that under the rules for accredited certification, consultancy cannot be provided during any pre-assessment offered by the Certification Body that will later undertake the certification audit.

3 Selection of an Audit Option

There are a number of options and processes available for sites to demonstrate their commitment to the *Global Standard for Food Safety*.

3.1   Enrolment programme

This is most suitable for companies that are either new to the Standard or are not yet certificated. The registration for enrolment is carried out by the Certification Body with the BRC on behalf of the company and enables access to information provided by the BRC on the Standards. The audit is undertaken at a date agreed with the Certification Body and could lead if successful to certification. It is recognised that many sites need a little time to develop their food safety systems and culture to meet the full BRC certification requirements. The enrolment programme allows for the generation of an audit report and score card which can be shared by customers and can be used to demonstrate the progressive development of the food safety system.

Details of the enrolment programme can be found on page 81.

3.2   Announced audit programme

This is available for existing certificated sites and is the same audit process used for sites within the enrolment programme. The audit date is agreed with the Certification Body in advance of the audit and all requirements of the Standard are audited within the audit visit. This has been the most commonly selected certification audit type and was used for most audits carried out against previous issues of the Standard.

Successful sites are awarded a certificate with the grade A, B or C depending on the number and type of non-conformities identified. However, the top grade of A$^+$ is not available with this audit option.

3.3   Unannounced audit programme

The unannounced audit options are only available to sites that have already been certificated to the Standard and have been awarded a grade A$^+$, A, B$^+$ or B.

The unannounced audit options provide sites with the opportunity to demonstrate the maturity of their quality systems and successful sites are awarded grades of A$^+$ (the top BRC grade), B$^+$ or C$^+$. The conducting of an independent, unannounced review of systems and procedures under this scheme provides a company's customers with added confidence in the company's ability to consistently maintain standards. This may influence the frequency of customer audits, where conducted, and other performance procedures applied by the customer.

There are two options for unannounced audits, which allows companies to decide the one best suited to their business requirements; the grading and reporting for each is the same. With both options the date of the audit of the factory good manufacturing processes (GMPs) is unannounced.

For option 1, the whole Standard is audited on a single unannounced audit visit, typically lasting two days.

For option 2, the audit visit is split into two separate visits, each typically lasting one day. The first visit, which is unannounced, audits predominantly factory GMPs, as highlighted by the colour-coding system in the Standard requirements. The second part of the audit, which is planned, audits predominantly the documented systems and records. This approach allows companies to ensure that appropriate managers are available to assist with the audit of documentation.

Details of the features of the unannounced audit options can be found on page 74.

4   Selection of a Certification Body

Once a self-assessment has been completed and non-conformities addressed, the company must select a Certification Body. The BRC cannot advise on the selection of a specific Certification Body; all BRC approved Certification Bodies are listed at www.brcdirectory.com.

In selecting a Certification Body, the company should consider the scope of the accreditation of the Certification Body. It is essential that the Certification Body is accredited to assess companies for the categories of products produced. Clarification of the categories of products against which the Certification Body can audit should be obtained either by confirmation from the Certification Body concerned or from accreditation schedules published by the appropriate national accreditation body. A list of product categories is provided in Appendix 4.

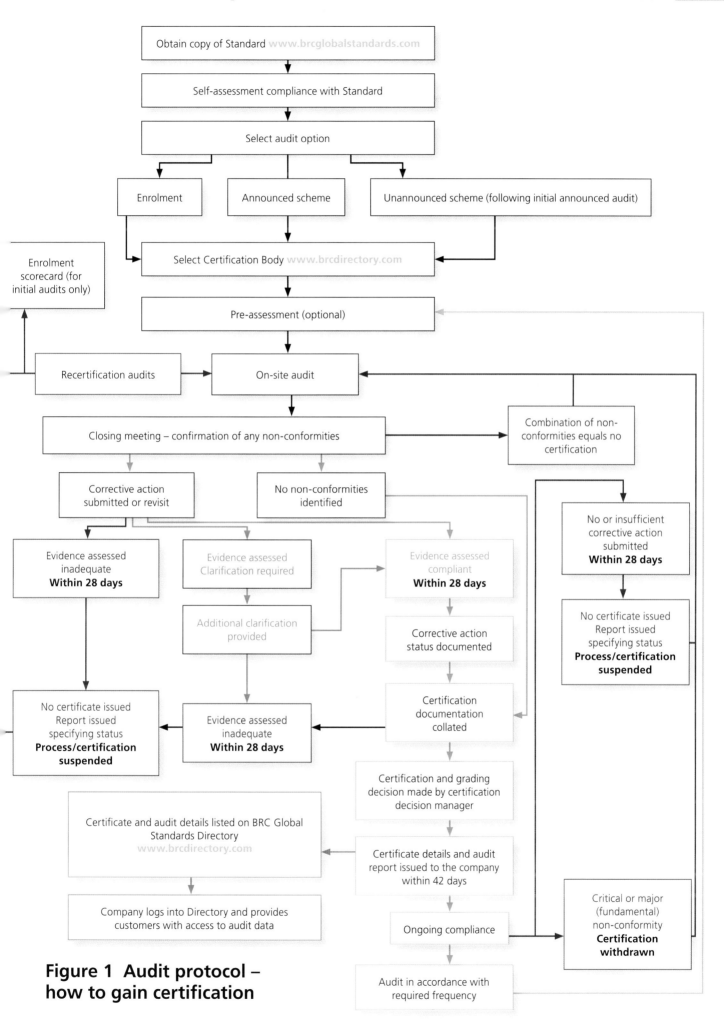

**Figure 1 Audit protocol –
how to gain certification**

5   Company/Certification Body Contractual Arrangements

A contract shall exist between the company and the Certification Body, detailing the scope of the audit and the reporting requirements. This Standard sets out the requirements for sites that want to apply to be audited against the Standard and for sites issued with a certificate. Contracts between the Certification Body and the site shall include a clause acknowledging these obligations. This contract will be formulated by the Certification Body.

The contract shall clearly identify that a copy of the audit report and any subsequent certificate or audit result shall be supplied to the BRC in the agreed format. The contract shall also dictate that all documents in relation to the audit shall be made available to the BRC upon request. Documents provided to the BRC will be treated as confidential.

5.1   Registration fee

The BRC will require a registration fee to be collected by the Certification Body from the company for every audit undertaken. The certificate and audit report shall not be valid until the registration fee and the Certification Body's audit fees have been received, irrespective of the outcome of the certification process.

6   Scope of Audit

6.1   Defining the audit scope

The scope of the audit – products produced and manufacturing processes – shall be agreed between the company and the Certification Body in advance of the audit to ensure the allocation of an auditor with the correct category and product knowledge. The audit shall include all applicable requirements within the Standard and all production processes undertaken at the site seeking certification, for the products within the defined scope of certification.

The audit scope and any permitted exclusions shall be clearly defined both on the audit report and on any certificate issued. The wording of the scope will be verified by the auditor during the site audit. The description of product groups and type of pack within the scope shall enable a recipient of the report or certificate to clearly identify whether products supplied have been included within the scope. This shall include a description of processing activities undertaken at the site that fall within the scope of this Standard, where this adds clarity for the user of the report or certificate (e.g. the slicing and packing of cooked meats).

The audit report and certificate shall cover only products manufactured at the site which has been audited. Products purchased for resale by a site 'factored goods' cannot be included within the scope of the certificate. A description of the process for managing factored goods may be included within the audit report.

6.2   Additional locations and head office assessments

The audit scope is expected to be site specific. There are, however, exceptional circumstances where the activities are undertaken at more than one location and where these can be included within a single report and certificate. These include:

- the audit of a head office to review procedures controlled from head office
- the audit of more than one location where a single production process is carried out across two sites.

The detailed requirements for acceptance and management of such circumstances within the audit protocol are provided in Appendix 7.

Whilst the storage facilities on the same site as the production facility shall always be included within the audit of the site, it is not uncommon for sites to also own additional off-site storage facilities. Where additional storage facilities are owned and managed by the company in the vicinity of the production site (i.e. within a radius of 50 km), these shall be identified on the audit report and either audited as part of the site audit or specifically excluded.

6.3 Exclusions from scope

The fulfilment of the certification criteria relies on clear commitment from the site management to adopt the best practice principles outlined within the Standard and to the development of a food safety culture within the business. It follows therefore that the exclusion of products from the scope of certification shall only be accepted by exception.

The exclusion of products produced at a site will only be acceptable where the excluded products can be clearly differentiated from products within scope and make up a minority of the products produced at the site and:

■ the products are produced in a separate area of the factory

or

■ the products are produced on different production equipment, e.g. products packed in glass jars in a cannery.

Where exclusions are requested these shall be agreed with the Certification Body in advance of the audit. Exclusions shall be clearly stated on the audit report and certificate and the justification recorded on the audit report.

The certification of products must include audit of the entire process from raw material to end-product dispatch. It is not possible to exclude either parts of the process undertaken at the site or parts of the Standard. Where exclusions are accepted, the auditor shall assess any hazards presented by excluded areas or products (e.g. the introduction of allergens).

6.4 Extensions to scope

Once certification has been granted, any additional significant products manufactured or processes undertaken by the site that are required to be included in the scope of certification must be communicated to the Certification Body. The Certification Body shall assess the significance of the new products or processes and decide whether to conduct a site visit. The current certificate will be superseded by any new certificate issued, using the same expiry date as detailed on the original certificate. For full details of the assessment procedures for extensions to scope, see Appendix 8.

6.5 Auditor selection

It is the responsibility of the company to ensure that adequate and accurate information is given to the Certification Body, detailing the products it manufactures and the process technologies it uses, to enable the Certification Body to select an auditor with the required skills to undertake the audit. Auditors must be skilled to audit in the relevant product category, as listed in Appendix 4.

The Certification Body, auditors and the company must be aware of the need to avoid conflict of interest when arranging an auditor for the site visit. The company may decline the services of a particular auditor offered by the Certification Body. The same auditor is not permitted to undertake audits on more than three consecutive occasions at the same site.

7 Audit Planning

7.1 Preparation by the company

For initial audits the company shall agree a mutually convenient date, with due consideration given to the amount of work required to meet the requirements of the Standard.

Manufacturing units that are newly built or 'commissioned' must ensure that systems and procedures in place are compliant before an initial BRC audit is undertaken. It is at the discretion of the company when they wish to invite a Certification Body to carry out an audit; however, it is unlikely that full compliance can be satisfactorily demonstrated at an audit undertaken less than three months from commencement of operation.

This is likely to be the situation even where the site for certification uses quality systems developed by other certificated companies in the group. A company may wish to consider a pre-assessment towards the end of this three-month period.

There is a requirement on the company to be prepared for the audit, to have appropriate documentation for the auditor to assess and to have appropriate staff available at all times during the on-site audit.

The company shall ensure that for planned audits the production programme at the time of the audit covers products for the intended scope of the certification. Where possible, the widest range of these products shall be in production for the auditor to assess. Where the product range is large or diverse, the auditor has the discretion to continue the audit until sufficiently satisfied that the intended scope of the certification has been assessed. Where a significant production process is undertaken only during a different period of the year from the audit, a separate audit will be required to assess that production method.

7.2   Information to be provided to the Certification Body for audit preparation

The company shall supply the Certification Body with background information prior to the audit day to ensure the auditor is fully prepared and to provide the best opportunity for the audit to be completed efficiently. The information will be requested by the Certification Body and may include but is not limited to:

- a summary of critical control points (CCPs)
- the process flow diagram
- a simple site plan
- the management organisational chart
- the list of products or product groups included within the audit scope
- typical shift patterns
- production schedules, to allow audits to cover relevant processes, for example night-time manufacture or where production processes are not carried out each day
- recent quality issues, withdrawals or customer complaints and other relevant performance data.

The company shall make the previous year's audit report and certificate available to the Certification Body, where this is a contract with a new Certification Body.

The time to assess all documentation by the auditor and Certification Body is supplementary to the duration of the audit.

7.3   Duration of the audit

Before the audit takes place, the Certification Body shall indicate the approximate duration of the audit. The typical duration of an audit is two man days at the site. A calculator has been developed to assess the expected time required to undertake the audit of any particular site to ensure consistency and this shall be used as the basis for calculating the total audit duration. Full details can be found on the BRC Global Standards website www.brcglobalstandards.com.

The calculation for the audit duration is based on:

- the number of employees – as full time equivalent employees per main shift, including seasonal workers
- the size of the manufacturing facility – including storage facilities on site
- the number of HACCP studies included within scope – an HACCP study corresponds to a family of products with similar hazards and similar production technology for the purpose of the calculator.

It is recognised that other factors may also influence the calculation but are considered to be less significant and therefore shall not influence the audit duration by more than 30% from the total calculated audit time. These factors include:

- the complexity of the manufacturing process
- the number of product lines

- the layout and age of the site and impact on material flow
- the labour-intensity of processes
- communication difficulties, e.g. language
- the number of non-conformities recorded in the previous audit
- difficulties experienced during the audit that require further investigation
- the quality of company preparation, e.g. documentation, HACCP, QMS.

If additional storage facilities, locations or head office assessments are included within the audit process then additional time shall be allocated for this over and above that indicated in the audit calculator.

The calculation for audit duration shall determine the amount of time to be expected to undertake the audit at the site. Additional time will be required for the review of any documentary evidence provided and completion of the final audit report.

Deviation from the calculated audit timeframe must be justified and specified on the audit report.

In the event that the audit against this Standard is intended to be combined with other audit Standards, the total audit time shall be sufficient to fulfil the BRC protocols. Details of combined audits shall be specified on the audit report.

8   The On-site Audit

The on-site audit consists of the following seven stages:

- Opening meeting – to confirm the scope and process of the audit.
- Document review – a review of the documented HACCP and quality management systems.
- Traceability challenge – including a vertical audit of associated records of production.
- Production facility inspection – to review practical implementation of the systems, including observing product changeover procedures, and interview of personnel.
- Review of production facility inspection – to verify and conduct further documentation checks.
- Final review of findings by the auditor – preparation for the closing meeting.
- Closing meeting – to review audit findings with the company. (Note that non-conformities are subject to subsequent independent verification by the Certification Body management.)

The company will fully assist the auditor at all times. It is expected that at the opening and closing meetings those attending on behalf of the company will be senior managers who have the appropriate authority to ensure that corrective action can be progressed if non-conformities are found. The most senior operations manager on site or their nominated deputy shall be available at the audit and attend the opening and closing meetings.

The audit process gives emphasis to the practical implementation of food safety procedures and general GMPs. It is expected that at least 50% of the audit will be spent auditing production and site facilities, interviewing staff, observing processes and reviewing documentation in production areas with the relevant staff.

During the audit, detailed notes shall be made regarding the company's conformities and non-conformities against the Standard and these will be used as the basis for the audit report. The auditor shall assess the nature and severity of any non-conformity.

At the closing meeting, the auditor shall present his/her findings and discuss all non-conformities that have been identified during the audit, but shall not make comment on the likely outcome of the certification process. Information on the process and timescales for the company to provide evidence to the auditor of the corrective action to close non-conformities must be given. A written summary of the non-conformities discussed at the closing meeting will be documented by the auditor either at the closing meeting or within one working day after completion of the audit.

At the closing meeting the auditor shall provide the company with an explanation of the BRC Directory system, which allows secure access to audit data to both the client and their nominated customers.

The decision to award certification and the grade of the certificate will be determined independently by the Certification Body management, following a technical review of the audit report and the closing of non-conformities in the appropriate timeframe. The company will be informed of the certification decision following this review.

9   Non-conformities and Corrective Action

The level of non-conformity assigned by an auditor against a requirement of the Standard is an objective judgement with respect to severity and risk and is based on evidence collected and observations made during the audit. This is verified by the Certification Body management.

9.1   Non-conformities

There are three levels of non-conformity:

- Critical – where there is a critical failure to comply with a food safety or legal issue.

- Major – where there is a substantial failure to meet the requirements of a 'statement of intent' or any clause of the Standard or a situation is identified which would, on the basis of available objective evidence, raise significant doubt as to the conformity of the product being supplied.

- Minor – where a clause has not been fully met but, on the basis of objective evidence, the conformity of the product is not in doubt.

The objective of the audit is to provide a true reflection of the standard of the operation and level of conformity against the *Global Standard for Food Safety*. Consideration should therefore be given to awarding a single major non-conformity where minor non-conformities are repeatedly raised against a particular clause of the Standard. Clustering of a significant number of minor non-conformities against a clause and recording this as a single minor non-conformity is not permitted.

9.2   Procedures for handling non-conformities and corrective action

Following identification of any non-conformities during the audit, the company must undertake corrective action both to remedy the immediate issue and to undertake an analysis of the underlying cause of the non-conformity (root cause) and develop a corrective action plan to address the root cause.

The process for 'closing out' non-conformities depends upon the level of non-conformity and the numbers of non-conformities identified.

9.2.1   Critical non-conformities or a combination of non-conformities resulting in non-certification

In some circumstances the number or severity of non-conformities raised at the audit prevent the site from being certificated following that audit. This will be the case where:

- a critical non-conformity is raised

and/or

- a major non-conformity against the statement of intent of a fundamental clause is raised

and/or

- the number or type of non-conformities exceeds the limits for certification, as per Table 1.

The grading of non-conformities will be reviewed by the independent certification process of the Certification Body as soon as possible after the audit. Where the review confirms that a certificate cannot be awarded, the site will be required to undertake another full audit before assessment for certification.

Due to the nature and number of non-conformities, it is unlikely that these non-conformities can be addressed and fully effective improvements implemented and established within a 28-day period – although there may be some exceptions. Therefore, the re-audit shall not take place any earlier than 28 days from the audit date.

Where this occurs at a certificated site, certification must be immediately withdrawn.

It is a requirement of some customers that they shall be informed when their suppliers have a critical non-conformity identified or fail to gain certification. In such circumstances the company shall immediately inform its customers and make them fully aware of the circumstances. Information on the corrective actions to be taken in order to address the non-conformities will also be provided to customers where required.

9.2.2   Major and minor non-conformities

No certificate shall be issued until major and minor non-conformities have been demonstrated as having been corrected, either permanently or via a temporary solution that is acceptable to the Certification Body.

For each non-conformity raised, the site shall, in addition to undertaking the necessary immediate corrective action, undertake a review of the underlying cause (root cause) of the non-conformity. The root cause shall be identified and an action plan to correct this, including timescale, provided to the Certification Body. This shall be included in the audit report.

Close out of non-conformities can be achieved either by objective evidence being submitted to the Certification Body, such as updated procedures, records, photographs or invoices for work undertaken, or by the Certification Body undertaking a further on-site visit.

Where the number and level of non-conformities identified at the audit would result in a grade C or C⁺ being awarded, the closure of non-conformities shall be by means of a further site visit to review the action taken. This visit shall be within 28 calendar days of the audit if a certificate is to be issued.

If satisfactory evidence is not provided within the 28 calendar day period allowed for submission following the audit, certification will not be granted. The company will then require a further full audit in order to be considered for certification.

Non-conformities from the audit shall also be checked during the next site audit to verify effective close out of the non-conformities and their root cause. Where the correction has been ineffective then a non-conformity shall be raised against clause 1.1.10.

10   Grading of the Audit

The purpose of the certification grading system is to indicate to the user of the report the commitment of the company to continual compliance and will dictate the future audit frequency. The grade is dependent on the number and severity of the non-conformities identified at the time of the audit. Non-conformities are verified by a technical review process by the Certification Body management. If the review results in a change in the number and/or severity of non-conformities, the company shall be notified.

Table 1 Summary of grading criteria, action required and audit frequency

Grade	Critical or major non-conformity against the statement of intent of a fundamental requirement	Critical	Major	Minor	Corrective action	Audit frequency
A/A⁺				1 to 10	Objective evidence in 28 calendar days	12 months
B/B⁺				11 to 20	Objective evidence in 28 calendar days	12 months
B/B⁺			1	1 to 10	Objective evidence in 28 calendar days	12 months
C/C⁺				21 to 30	Revisit required within 28 calendar days	6 months
C/C⁺			1	11 to 30	Revisit required within 28 calendar days	6 months
C/C⁺			2	1 to 20	Revisit required within 28 calendar days	6 months
No Grade	1 or more				Certification not granted. Re-audit required	
No Grade		1 or more			Certification not granted. Re-audit required	
No Grade				31 or more	Certification not granted. Re-audit required	
No Grade			2	21 or more	Certification not granted. Re-audit required	
No Grade			3 or more		Certification not granted. Re-audit required	

Note. + grades only apply to unannounced audit schemes.

Certification will not be granted, and therefore no grade shall be awarded, if corrective action is not completed or sufficient evidence of completion is not received by the Certification Body within the 28 calendar-day timescale.

The Certification Body shall justify a high number (more than 20) of minor non-conformities where no more than one major non-conformity is given. This shall be detailed on the audit report.

The Certification Body will review objective evidence of corrective action completed prior to awarding a certificate, but this shall not change the grade awarded.

11   Audit Reporting

Following each audit, a full written report shall be prepared in the agreed format. The report shall be produced in English or in another language, dependent upon user needs. Where the report is produced in a language other than English, the audit summary sections shall, in addition, always be reported in English.

The audit report shall provide the company and customers or prospective customers with a profile of the company and an accurate summary of the performance of the company against the requirements of the Standard.

The audit report must assist the reader to be informed of:

- the food safety controls in place and improvements since the last audit
- 'best practice' systems, procedures, equipment or fabrication in place
- non-conformities, the corrective action taken and plans to correct the root cause.

The report shall accurately reflect the findings of the auditor during the audit. Reports shall be prepared and dispatched to the company within 42 calendar days of the completion of the full audit.

Audit reports shall remain the property of the company commissioning the audit and shall not be released, in whole or part, to a third party unless the company has given prior consent (unless otherwise required by law).

The audit report shall be uploaded onto the BRC Directory in a timely manner irrespective of whether a certificate is issued. The owner of the audit report may allocate access to the audit report to customers or other parties on the BRC Directory.

The audit report and associated documentation, including the auditor's notes, shall be stored safely and securely for a period of five years by the Certification Body.

12   Certification

After a review of the audit report and documentary evidence provided in relation to the non-conformities identified, a certification decision shall be made by the designated independent certification manager. Where a certificate is granted this shall be issued by the Certification Body within 42 calendar days of the audit. The certificate shall conform to the format shown in Appendix 5. Logos used on certificates (e.g. BRC and accreditation body logos) shall comply with their respective usage rules.

- The certificate will detail the scope of the audit and any accepted exclusions from scope.
- The certificate will clearly indicate the audit option chosen (i.e. announced, unannounced audit option 1 or 2), or whether the certificate is a reissue for an extension to scope.
- The certificate will include the six-digit auditor registration number of the lead auditor.
- The date(s) of audit specified on the certificate shall be the date of the audit relating to the granting of that certificate irrespective of whether later visits were made to verify corrective action arising from the audit.

Whilst the certificate is issued to the company, it remains the property of the Certification Body that controls its ownership, use and display.

13   BRC Logos and Plaques

Achieving BRC certification is something of which to be proud. Companies that achieve certification are qualified to use the BRC logo on company stationery and other marketing materials. A BRC wall plaque is available for certificated companies to display in their offices to help celebrate their success. Information and conditions relating to the use of the BRC logo is available at www.brcglobalstandards.com.

If a site is no longer certificated because of certificate expiry, withdrawal or suspension they shall no longer use the logo or display any plaque or certificate claiming certification.

The BRC logo is not a product certification mark and shall not be used on products or product packaging. Any certificated site found to be misusing the mark will be subject to the BRC complaints/referral process (see page 88) and may risk suspension or removal of their certification.

14   The BRC Global Standards Directory

14.1 Introduction

The Global Standards Directory www.brcdirectory.com is an online searchable directory of companies certificated to the BRC Global Standards for food safety, packaging, consumer products and storage and distribution. Each entry includes relevant site details, and contact and certification information. The directory also includes details of Certification Bodies approved by the BRC.

The Global Standards Directory was developed to publicise the list of certificated companies, provide key information to retailers and other specifiers and improve the management of the BRC Global Standards programme. It provides a system of data storage of audit information, both live and archived. Data is centrally managed and controlled to maintain accuracy and integrity.

14.2 Directory functionality

Information about certificated companies is provided to the BRC by Certification Bodies. The Directory provides the following publicly available facilities:

- a searchable list of certificated companies, including contact details, the Standard against which they are certified, scope and links to their website
- a searchable list of approved Certification Bodies, including local offices and contact details.

Note that whilst all reports and certificate details shall be uploaded onto the Directory, companies may choose not to appear on the public directory site if they so wish; this will not, however, exempt sites from the registration fee.

The Global Standards Directory provides additional functionality to key user groups, including companies, retailers and Certification Bodies. This includes user-specific access to certification information, audit reports and management reporting, further enhancing the value of obtaining BRC certification.

15   Surveillance of Certificated Companies

For certificated companies, where appropriate, the Certification Body or the BRC may carry out further audits, or question activities to validate continued certification, at any time. These visits may take the form of announced or unannounced visits to undertake either a full or part audit.

Any non-conformities identified at a visit must be corrected and closed out within the normal protocol (i.e. within 28 days of the visit), and reviewed and accepted by the Certification Body. If there is no intention on behalf of the company to take appropriate corrective actions or the corrective actions are deemed inappropriate, certification shall be withdrawn. The ultimate decision to suspend or withdraw certification remains with the Certification Body. Any change in certification status shall be notified to the BRC by the Certification Body and the status on the BRC Directory amended accordingly.

In the event that certification is withdrawn or suspended by the Certification Body, the company shall immediately inform its customers and make them fully aware of the circumstances relating to the withdrawal or suspension. Information on the corrective actions to be taken in order to reinstate certification status will also be provided to customers.

16 Ongoing Audit Frequency and Certification

16.1 Scheduling re-audit dates

The ongoing audit schedule and choice of audit programme will be agreed between the company and the Certification Body. The frequency of announced audits will be 6 or 12 months and is dependent upon the performance of the company at an audit as reflected by the grade (refer to Table 1). Unannounced audit frequencies are determined by the programme requirements.

The due date of the subsequent audit shall be calculated from the date of the initial audit, irrespective of whether further site visits were made to verify corrective action arising from the audit, and not from the certificate issue date.

The subsequent announced audit shall be scheduled to occur within a 28-day time period up to the next audit due date. This allows sufficient time for corrective action to take place in the event of any non-conformities being raised, without jeopardising continued certification.

Appendix 6 provides worked examples in accordance with the 6-month and 12-month audit frequencies.

It is the responsibility of the company to maintain certification. Where an audit is delayed beyond the due date, except in justifiable circumstances, this shall result in a major non-conformity being awarded at the next audit. Justifiable circumstances shall be documented in the audit report.

16.2 Delayed audits – justifiable circumstances

There will be some circumstances where the certificate cannot be renewed on the 6-month or 12-month basis due to the inability of the Certification Body to conduct an audit. These justifiable circumstances, which would not result in the assigning of a major non-conformity (refer to Section II, clause 1.1.8), can include when the site is:

- situated in a specific country or an area within a specific country where there is government advice to not visit and there is no suitable local auditor
- within a statutory exclusion zone that could compromise food safety or animal welfare
- in an area that has suffered a natural or unnatural disaster, rendering the site unable to produce or the auditor unable to visit.

Moving the audit date to a more 'acceptable' later date for reasons of combining audits, lack of personnel or undertaking building work is not an acceptable reason for missing the due date.

If the renewal of the certificate is prevented due to these exceptional circumstances, the customer may still decide to take products from that site for an agreed time, as they may still demonstrate legal compliance by other means, such as risk assessment and complaints records, to show that the site is still competent to continue production until another audit can be arranged.

16.3 Audits undertaken prior to due dates

In some circumstances it is possible to undertake the audit earlier than the due dates, for example to reset the audit dates to allow combined audits with another scheme, or to include a product produced at a different season. Where an audit date is brought forward the following rules shall apply:

- The audit report will detail the reasons why an audit has been brought forward.
- The audit due date will be 'reset' to be 12 months (or 6 months depending on grade) from this audit date.

■ The certificate should be issued with an expiry date of 12 months (or 6 months, depending on grade) + 42 days from the 'new' audit date.

16.4 Seasonal production sites

Refer to Glossary for the definition of 'seasonal production sites'.

Audits must be carried out when the site is in production to enable all requirements of the standard to be assessed. The actual audit date is likely to be dictated by product harvest, which may be affected by the weather. There is no penalty for the delay in audit date where this is the result of a late season for such sites, although the justification for the delay must be included on the report.

Where a site is awarded a Grade C, it is likely that the site will not be in production when the audit would normally be due 6 months later. In such circumstances the next audit shall take place once production has started in the new season.

Seasonal production sites may opt for the unannounced programmes although special rules operate as defined in the programmes.

17   Communication with Certification Bodies

In the event that any circumstances change within the company that may affect the validity of continuing certification, the company must immediately notify the Certification Body. These may include:

■ legal proceedings with respect to product safety or legality

■ product recall

■ significant damage to the site, e.g. natural disaster such as flood or damage by fire

■ change of ownership.

The Certification Body in turn shall take appropriate steps to assess the situation and any implications for the certification, and shall take any appropriate action.

Information shall be provided to the Certification Body by the site on request so that an assessment can be made as to the effect on the validity of the current certificate.

The Certification Body may as appropriate:

■ confirm the validity of certification

■ suspend certification pending further investigation

■ require further details of corrective action taken by the company

■ undertake a site visit to verify the control of processes and confirm continued certification

■ withdraw certification

■ issue a new certificate with the new owners' details.

Changes to the certification status of a company shall be recorded on the BRC Directory.

18   Appeals

The company has the right to appeal the certification decision made by the Certification Body and any appeal should be made in writing to the Certification Body within seven calendar days of receipt of the certification decision.

The Certification Body shall have a documented procedure for the consideration and resolution of appeals against the certification decision. These investigative procedures shall be independent of the individual auditor and certification manager. Individual Certification Bodies' documented appeals procedures will be made available to the company on request. Appeals will be finalised within 30 calendar days of receipt. A full written response will be given after the completion of a full and thorough investigation into the appeal.

In the event of an unsuccessful appeal, the Certification Body has the right to charge costs for conducting the appeal.

Part 2 – Audit Protocol for Specific Programmes

The Announced Audit Programme

1   Announced Audit

1.1   Eligibility

The announced audit programme is open to all certificated companies and for sites in the enrolment programme.

1.2   Benefits

The audits are always planned in advance between the Certification Body and the site, which enables the company to prepare for the audit by ensuring that:

- a date is selected when the maximum number of products within the scope are in production
- relevant managers and, where appropriate, consultants can be available for the audit
- the site can review its systems and procedures in preparation for the audit.

1.3   Features of the audit programme

The audit and certification process operates to the rules set out in the protocol. Grades awarded at certification are limited to A, B and C grades.

Should existing certificated sites fail to gain a certificate on re-audit no certificate is issued; however, existing certificated sites do not enter the enrolment programme. Sites will be expected to have a re-audit to regain certification.

The Unannounced Audit Programmes

Two unannounced audit programmes are available. Figure 2 shows the certification process.

2   Option 1 – Full Unannounced Audit

This option involves a single unannounced audit against all of the requirements of the Standard.

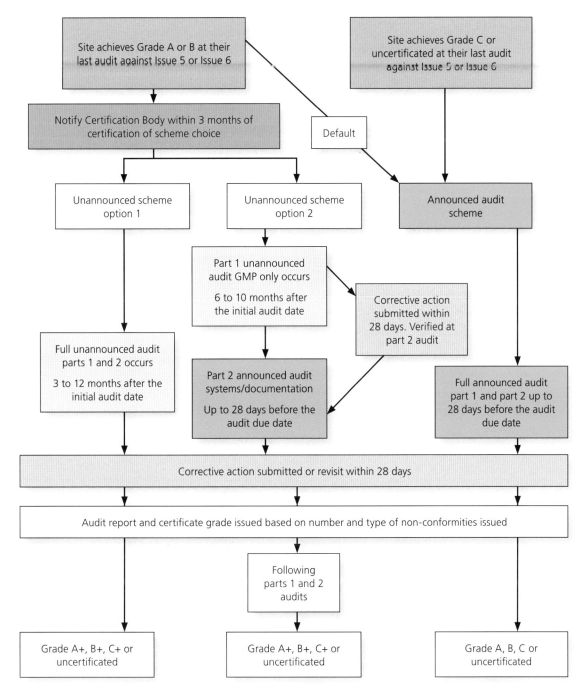

Figure 2 Unannounced audit scheme – certification process

2.1 Eligibility

Participation in the unannounced audit programme is voluntary. The programme is only open to those sites that are currently awarded a certification Grade A+, A, B+ or B, following their audit against either Issue 5 or Issue 6 of the Standard.

The decision to join the programme shall be made within the first three months following a qualifying audit. After this period only the announced scheme will be available (this provides the opportunity for sites to change Certification Body if they wish).

The scheme is also available to sites producing seasonally.

2.2   Benefits

The programme provides a company's customers with the knowledge that an independent, unannounced review of its systems and procedures is undertaken and is therefore a further means by which they can assess their risk rating of suppliers. This may influence the frequency of customer audit, where conducted, and other performance procedures applied by the customer.

Certification against the unannounced audit programme demonstrates confidence in a company's management of food safety.

Certification against the unannounced audit programme allows successful sites to achieve A+, B+ or C+ grades. The A+ is the top grade available under the Standard.

2.3   How the programme operates

2.3.1   Selection of the unannounced audit option 1 programme

If a site is eligible to apply for and wishes to join the unannounced audit programme, they shall notify their Certification Body within three months of their last audit date. This allows the opportunity for the site to select an alternative Certification Body if required whilst enabling the audit to be undertaken at a time of the Certification Body's choosing.

The option 1 programme allows for a number of days (up to 15) to be blocked out from the audit plan as non-audit days. This is to accommodate dates where an audit would be inappropriate and may include, for example, periods of planned factory shut down, short periods of refurbishment or planned customer visits. Any such blocked dates shall be notified to the Certification Body at the time of opting for the unannounced audit programme.

Certification bodies are expected to operate discretion in the case of emergencies.

It is a condition of electing to join the unannounced scheme that the auditor shall be granted access to the site for the audit on arrival. If access is denied the site will be liable for the auditor's costs and will revert to the announced audit scheme. At the discretion of the Certification Body, the existing certificate may also be suspended or withdrawn.

2.3.2   Audit planning

Sufficient information shall have been provided to the Certification Body when selecting this option to allow for the selection of an auditor with the correct category qualifications and to allow sufficient time for the audit. The audit duration shall be calculated using the BRC audit calculator and the same time shall be allowed for the unannounced audit as would be expected for the usual announced audit.

The audit will be unannounced and replace the normal scheduled audit. Although this may occur at any stage between months 3 and 12 of the audit due date, this shall typically be within the last four months of the certification cycle.

The date of the audit shall not be notified to the site in advance of the audit. Sites opting for the unannounced scheme shall be obliged to accommodate the auditor and allow the audit to start immediately on arrival at the site.

2.3.3   Audit process

The audit process will follow the same procedures as outlined in section 8. It is expected, however, that the audit will always begin with the site production facility inspection and this will be expected to commence within 30 minutes of the auditor arriving on site.

2.3.4   Grading and certification

The processes for reporting and correcting non-conformities shall be the same as described within the general audit protocol.

The grade awarded following certification shall be based on the number and level of non-conformities, as outlined in Table 1, except that the grade will have the addition of a + after the grade (i.e. A+, B+ or C+).

The audit report and certificate will state 'Unannounced option 1'. This certificate will supersede the existing certificate. The certificate shall be issued within 42 days of the audit and will have an expiry date based on the expiry date of the previous certificate plus 12 months, providing the company remains within the unannounced audit scheme. If the company decides to return to the announced audit programme, the certificate expiry date will be based 6 or 12 months from the date of the unannounced audit.

This ensures that where the audit occurs before the expiry of the current certificate and the company remains within the unannounced scheme, it is not disadvantaged by a shorter certificate life and increased frequency of audits. Appendix 6 provides worked examples of audit and certificate expiry dates.

2.3.5   Planning the next audit

If an A$^+$ or B$^+$ grade is achieved at the audit, the company can choose whether to:

- remain within the option 1 programme
- transfer to the unannounced option 2 programme
- revert to the announced audit programme.

If the site achieves a grade C$^+$, the next audit will automatically revert to the announced audit programme.

If the company wishes to remain in the option 1 programme the next audit will be unannounced and will occur as indicated by the audit planning rules above. The audit dates will be based on the certificate expiry date.

If the company opts to move to the unannounced option 2 programme, the rules for that programme will apply and the announced systems audit will occur within the 28-day window based on the initial audit date.

If the company wishes to withdraw from the unannounced audit programme, the next audit will be scheduled to occur within the 28 days up to and including the anniversary of the last audit date; this ensures that the maximum time between audits is not more than a year.

2.3.6   Seasonal production sites

The option 1 unannounced programme may be applied to seasonal production sites. The following rules will, however, apply:

- The expected seasonal production dates shall be notified to the Certification Body at the time of choosing the unannounced scheme.
- No dates may be excluded within the production season.

3   Option 2 – Two-Part Unannounced Audit

The option 2 unannounced audit scheme divides the audit requirements into two separate audits. The first audit looks predominantly at the issues considered to be factory-based GMPs and is carried out as an unannounced audit. The second audit is predominantly based on reviewing documentation and records and can be planned to ensure the appropriate management staff are available to retrieve and discuss the records.

The requirements of the Standard are colour coded to identify the requirements which would be audited during different audit visits.

3.1   Eligibility

Participation in the unannounced audit programme is voluntary and only open to those sites that are currently awarded a certification Grade A$^+$, A, B$^+$ or B, following their audit against either Issue 5 or Issue 6 of the Standard.

The decision to join the programme shall be made within the first three months following a qualifying audit. After this period only the announced scheme will be available (this provides the opportunity for sites to change Certification Body if they wish).

The scheme is also available to sites producing seasonally; however, separate rules will apply.

3.2 Benefits

The programme provides a company's customers with the knowledge that an independent, unannounced review of its systems and procedures is undertaken and is therefore a further means by which they can assess their risk rating of suppliers. This may influence the frequency of customer audit, where conducted, and other performance procedures applied by the customer.

Certification against the unannounced audit programme demonstrates confidence in a company's management of food safety and allows successful sites to achieve A+, B+ or C+ grades. The A+ is the top grade available under the Standard.

The two-part unannounced audit scheme allows the site to ensure the availability of managers for the documentation and systems – part 2 – audit. The planned part 2 audit allows this part of the audit to be combined with other planned certification audits where these are used to reduce audit costs.

3.3 How the programme operates

3.3.1 Selection of the unannounced audit option 2 programme

If a site is eligible to apply for the unannounced audit programme and wishes to join the programme, they shall notify their Certification Body within three months of their last audit date. This allows the opportunity for the site to select an alternative Certification Body if required whilst allowing the audit to be undertaken at a time of the Certification Body's choosing.

The option 2 programme allows for a number of days (up to 10) to be blocked out from the audit plan as non-audit days. This is to accommodate dates where an audit would be inappropriate and may include, for example, periods of planned factory shut down, short periods of refurbishment or planned customer visits. Any such blocked dates shall be notified to the Certification Body at the time of opting for the unannounced audit programme.

Certification bodies are expected to operate discretion in the case of emergencies.

It is a condition of electing to join the unannounced scheme that the auditor shall be granted access to the site for the audit on arrival. If access is denied the site will be liable for the auditor's costs and will revert to the announced audit scheme. At the discretion of the Certification Body, the existing certificate may also be suspended or withdrawn.

3.3.2 Audit planning

Sufficient information shall have been provided to the Certification Body when selecting this option to allow for the appointment of an auditor with the correct category qualifications and to allow sufficient time for the audit. The audit duration shall be calculated using the BRC audit calculator. The total audit time as determined by the calculator should be divided equally between the two audit visits. Typically one day should be allowed for each of the part 1 and the part 2 audits.

The unannounced part 1 audit shall occur at any stage between months 6 and 10 of the audit cycle (i.e. 2 to 6 months before the audit due date). This allows sites to correct any non-conformities identified at the audit to enable these to be reviewed at the part 2 audit.

The site may nominate up to 10 days at the time of selecting this unannounced scheme when the audit cannot occur. This is to cover known plant shut downs and avoid clashes with planned customer visits.

The part 2 audit of documentation and records shall be planned to occur in the 28 days up to and including the anniversary of the last audit date (i.e. in the same time window as an announced audit). The date for this audit is agreed with the site in advance of the audit.

3.3.3 Part 1 – Unannounced 'good manufacturing process' based audit

3.3.3.1 Audit process

The audit will start with a short opening meeting with the site management to confirm the plans for the audit and will normally proceed to the production facility inspection within 30 minutes of arrival.

The audit will primarily cover the factory operations (GMP) section indicated as part 1 requirements of the Standard (indicated in key colour coding below), but may call on supporting documentation normally covered in a part 2 audit where required to complete an audit trail.

Key to colour coding of requirements:

Requirements assessed on part 1 – audit of good manufacturing practice		
Requirements assessed on both part 1 and part 2		

3.3.3.2 Non-conformities and corrective actions

At the end of the audit the auditor will confirm any non-conformities identified during the process. Non-conformities raised during the audit shall be corrected and a plan defined to identify the root cause of the non-conformance. The corrective action and plan to address the root cause shall be provided to the Certification Body, within 28 days of the audit date, for review.

The non-conformities and their corrective action from the part 1 audit will be reviewed on site as part of the part 2 audit. The non-conformities will however count towards the audit grade even where fully corrected before the completion of the audit.

If a critical non-conformity and/or the number and level of non-conformities identified at the part 1 audit would result in the failure to achieve a certificate, the existing certificate for the site shall be immediately withdrawn.

3.3.3.3 Reporting process

A report detailing any non-conformities identified shall be provided to the site within two working days of the audit (this would usually be provided at the end of the audit).

During the audit the auditor shall record information identifying how a site complies with requirements of the Standard and this will be recorded in the final audit report completed after the part 2 audit.

Unless there is a need to withdraw the site's certificate, the current certificate will remain in place and any new certificate will not be issued until part 2 is completed.

3.3.4 Part 2 – Announced audit of systems and documentation

3.3.4.1 Audit timing

The audit shall be arranged with the site to be carried out in the 28-day window up to and including the audit due date indicated on the certificate. The audit date shall be agreed with the site and a plan prepared for the audit visit.

3.3.4.2 Audit process

The audit will cover primarily systems and documentation, as indicated as part 2 of the requirements of the Standard (indicated in key colour coding below). The audit will however include a factory tour to review any non-conformities arising from the part 1 audit, gather data to inform the document review and ensure that appropriate standards of GMP are maintained.

Correction of non-conformities identified during the part 1 audit shall be verified during the audit.

Key to colour coding of requirements:

Requirements assessed on part 2 – audit of records, systems and documentation		
Requirements assessed on both part 1 and part 2		

3.3.4.3 Non-conformities and corrective actions

Non-conformities identified at the part 2 audit shall be notified to the site management and confirmed at the closing meeting. The non-conformities from the part 1 and the part 2 audits shall be added together to decide the final grade. If a critical non-conformity is identified, the certificate for the site shall be immediately withdrawn.

Major and minor non-conformities shall be corrected and documentary evidence provided to the Certification Body within 28 days of the audit, together with action plans to address the root cause of the non-conformity.

3.3.5   Final audit report

A full audit report shall be produced in the standard format following completion of the part 2 audit. The report will include all non-conformities identified at both the part 1 and the part 2 audits and the corrective action taken. The final report will include information identifying how the site complied with the requirements of both the part 1 and the part 2 audits.

3.3.6   Grading and certification

The grade will be based upon the total number and level of non-conformities raised during both the part 1 and the part 2 audits, using the grade system outlined in Table 1, except that the grade will have the addition of a + after the grade (i.e. A⁺, B⁺ or C⁺).

The audit report and any certificate awarded will state 'Unannounced option 2'. The certificate shall be issued within 42 days of the completion of the part 2 audit and will have an expiry date based on the expiry date of the previous certificate plus 6 or 12 months depending on the grade awarded. The next audit due date on the certificate will be based on the initial audit date and will apply to the part 2 audit.

3.3.7   Planning the next audit

If an A⁺ or B⁺ grade is achieved at the audit the company can choose whether to:

- remain within the option 2 programme
- transfer to the unannounced option 1 programme
- revert to the announced audit programme. If the site achieves a grade C⁺, the next audit will automatically revert to the announced audit programme.

If the company wishes to remain in the option 2 programme, the audits will be undertaken as indicated by the audit planning rules above.

If the company opts to move to unannounced option 1, the rules for that programme will apply and the full unannounced audit will occur between 3 and 12 months after the initial audit date.

If the company wishes to withdraw from the unannounced audit programme, the next audit will be scheduled to occur within the 28 days up to and including the audit due date indicated on the certificate.

3.3.8   Seasonal production sites

The option 2 unannounced programme may be applied to seasonal production sites. The following rules will, however, apply.

- The expected seasonal production dates shall be notified to the Certification Body at the time of choosing the unannounced scheme.
- No dates may be excluded within the production season.
- Where the option 2 scheme is chosen, the documentation and systems audit will take place at a pre-arranged date at least 28 days before the expected start to the season to allow for completion of any corrective actions. The part 1 GMP audit will be carried out as an unannounced audit during the season.

The Enrolment Programme

The full enrolment process is shown in Figure 3.

4 Details of the Enrolment Programme

4.1 Eligibility

The enrolment process is designed for companies who have not previously been certificated to Issue 5 or Issue 6 of the Standard.

4.2 Benefits

The programme provides an introduction to the BRC certification process and the score attached to the audit allows sites and their customers to monitor the progress of the site towards eventual certification.

The audit process itself provides a structure to the development of a company's food safety system. Sites that are not yet at a standard for certification are able to use the BRC Directory to provide audit reports for their customers against an internationally recognised Standard.

4.3 How the programme operates

The audit programme will operate in exactly the same way as for sites seeking certification. A full audit of the site will be carried out in accordance with the process outlined in detail within the protocol sections 4 to 9.

Sites wanting to be part of the programme shall be registered on the BRC Directory by their chosen Certification Body and the proposed audit date entered onto the system. This ensures that the audit result can be recognised by the BRC.

4.3.1 The audit

A complete audit is carried out by a fully trained and BRC-registered auditor, competent in the category of products produced by the site as defined in their scope.

The audit duration is based on the audit duration calculator and typically lasts two days. The audit date is planned between the Certification Body and the site.

4.3.2 Non-conformities

The auditor completes the audit and categorises any non-conformities with the requirements as critical, major or minor and describes them in detail.

If the site has performed well and received fewer non-conformities than the number that prevents certification, they may decide to progress to certification. In this case, they must close out any non-conformities and provide an action plan to address the root cause of the non-conformity within the allowed period (28 calendar days following the visit). An action plan and documentary evidence must be provided to the Certification Body who will make the certification decision. If this is positive, the site will be awarded certification and receive the appropriate grade (refer to Table 1, page 68).

If the site does not achieve certification, either because of too many non-conformities or because the non-conformities were not closed out within the allowed timeframe, the site enters the continual development phase.

An audit scorecard is created and the audit report and scorecard are uploaded onto the BRC Directory within 42 days.

4.3.3 Scoring

The BRC has developed a scoring system for sites which have not achieved certification which is based on the number and type of non-conformities identified at the audit.

The BRC recognises the value of the GFSI (refer to Glossary) programme for the development of food safety standards and, in line with this, the score is weighted to correspond with the Basic and Intermediate level requirements within the GFSI programme.

The auditor will raise non-conformities and categorise as minor, major or critical. Each clause of the Standard is scored. Each non-conformity results in 'penalty points', which are deducted from a possible maximum score. The scores are subtotalled, resulting in a score for each of the seven requirements sections of the Standard and combined to give an overall audit score.

The objective of the score is to help the site to identify the areas for improvement and to demonstrate to customers a continually improving score as the site progresses towards full certification.

For sites in continual development, a scorecard is posted on the Directory showing the overall scores as well as those for individual sections.

If a site meets the requirements and achieves certification then it is no longer in the development phase and does not have a score. Instead, it has a certification grade which is dependent on its level of compliance during the audit.

4.3.4   Corrective action/improvement plans

Sites in the 'continual development' phase are expected to provide a corrective action or improvement plan within 28 calendar days of the audit, which will be reviewed by the Certification Body. The action plan shall be included within the audit report and will be posted on the Directory by the Certification Body. This information is for the benefit of the company and their customers only and is not verified or assessed by the BRC.

It is not possible for a site in the continual development phase to change their score or to achieve certification without a further audit. For a site to move from 'continual development' to 'certificated' status a complete re-audit must occur.

4.3.5   Directory listing and status

The BRC Directory has both a secure login accessible area and public site. Listings on the public site are restricted to certificated sites only and only contain a summary of the certification information.

The audit report details and scorecard for sites in the enrolment process will be available on the private area of the BRC Directory. Sites can make the information available to their customers on this area.

4.3.6   Planning the next audit

Certificated sites must follow the schedule for re-audit visits depending on the grade achieved (refer to section 16). Sites in the continual development phase must have another audit visit within 12 months of the initial (or any subsequent) audits. If, however, a site considers that it is ready for certification, there is no obligation to wait for 12 months and a re-audit can be arranged at any time.

If an audit does not take place within any 12-month period, the site details will be automatically removed from the BRC Directory and any customers selected to receive information about the site will be informed.

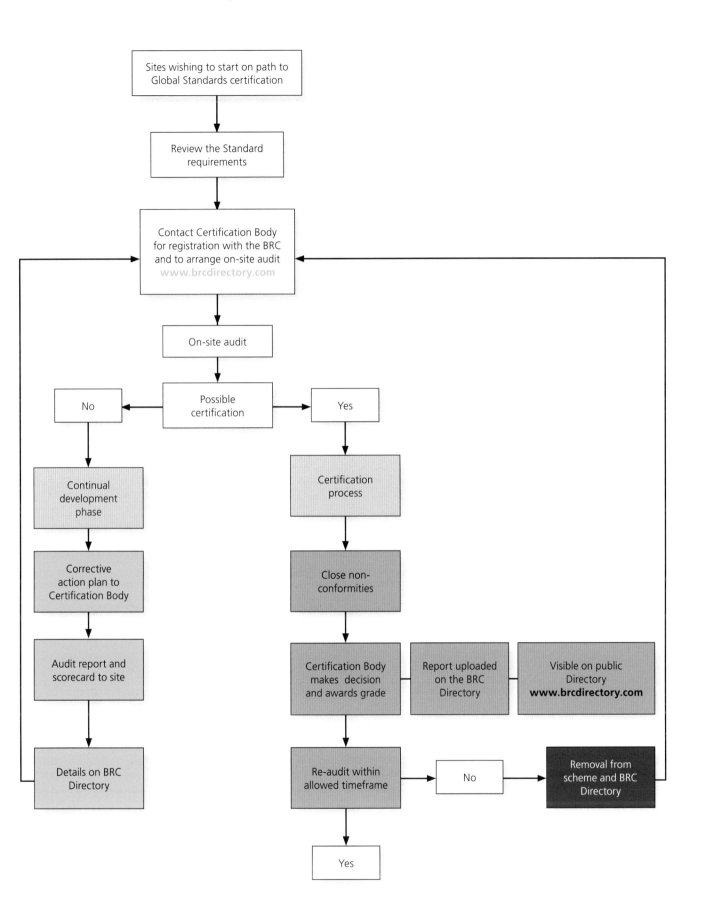

Figure 3 Enrolment process

SECTION IV

MANAGEMENT AND GOVERNANCE OF THE SCHEME

Section IV

Management and Governance of the Scheme

1   Requirements for Certification Bodies

The *Global Standard for Food Safety* is a process and product certification scheme. In this scheme, businesses are certificated upon completion of a satisfactory audit by an auditor employed by an independent third party – the Certification Body. The Certification Body in turn shall have been assessed and judged as competent by a national accreditation body.

The process of certification and accreditation is outlined in Figure 4.

In order for a business to receive a valid certificate on completion of a satisfactory audit, the organisation must select a Certification Body approved by the BRC. The BRC lays down detailed requirements that a Certification Body must satisfy in order to gain approval.

As a minimum, the Certification Body must be accredited to ISO/IEC Guide 65/EN45011 by a national accreditation body affiliated to the International Accreditation Forum and recognised by the BRC.

Further details are available in the document 'Requirements for Organisations Offering Certification against the Criteria of the BRC Global Standards', which is available from the BRC on request.

Companies looking to become certificated to the Standard should assure themselves that they are using a genuine Certification Body approved by the BRC. A list of all Certification Bodies approved by the BRC is available on the BRC Global Standards Directory: www.brcdirectory.com

The BRC recognises that in certain circumstances, such as for new Certification Bodies wishing to commence auditing against the Standard, accreditation may not yet have been achieved. This is because the accreditation process itself requires some audits to have been completed which will then be reviewed as part of the Accreditation audit of the Certification Body. The Certification Body must be able to conduct audits as part of the process of achieving accreditation and so some unaccredited audits will be performed. This will be permitted where the organisation can demonstrate:

- an active application for accreditation against ISO/IEC Guide 65/EN45011 from an approved national accreditation body

- that accreditation will be achieved within 12 months of the date of application and the experience and qualifications of the auditors in the relevant product category are consistent with those specified by the BRC

- a contract is in place with the BRC and all other contracted requirements have been met.

The acceptability of audit reports generated by Certification Bodies awaiting accreditation but meeting the above criteria is at the discretion of individual specifiers.

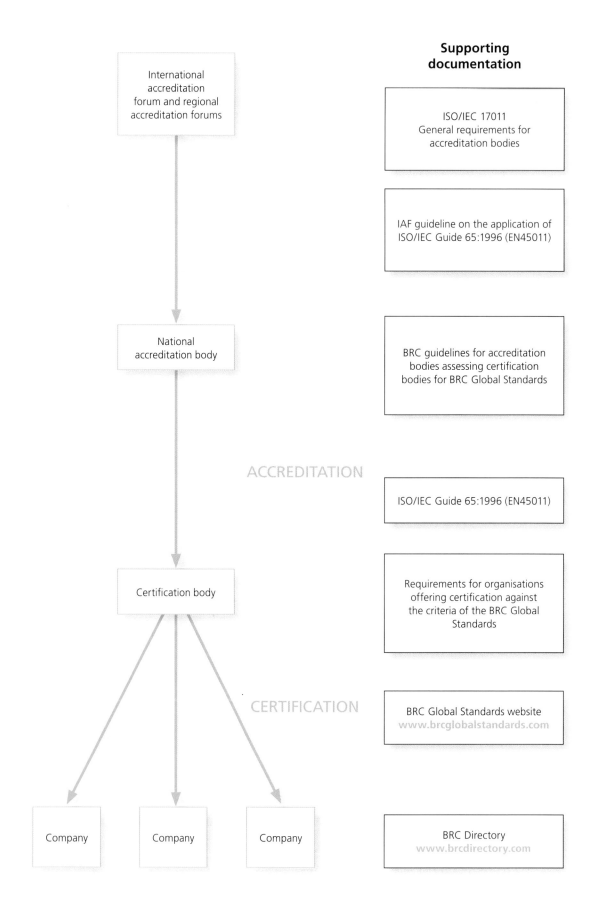

Supporting documentation

ISO/IEC 17011
General requirements for accreditation bodies

IAF guideline on the application of ISO/IEC Guide 65:1996 (EN45011)

BRC guidelines for accreditation bodies assessing certification bodies for BRC Global Standards

ISO/IEC Guide 65:1996 (EN45011)

Requirements for organisations offering certification against the criteria of the BRC Global Standards

BRC Global Standards website www.brcglobalstandards.com

BRC Directory www.brcdirectory.com

International accreditation forum and regional accreditation forums

National accreditation body

ACCREDITATION

Certification body

CERTIFICATION

Company

Company

Company

Figure 4 Process for accreditation of Certification Bodies

2 Technical Governance of the *Global Standard for Food Safety*

The Standard and associated scheme is managed by the BRC and is governed through a number of committees (Figure 5), each of which works to a set of defined terms of reference.

2.1 Governance and Strategy Committee

The technical management and operation of the Standard is governed by the BRC Governance and Strategy Committee, which consists of senior technical representatives of international retail and food manufacturing businesses.

The functions of the Governance and Strategy Committee are:

- to advise on the development and management of the Global Standards
- to ensure measures are in place to monitor compliance by companies, Certification Bodies and accreditation bodies
- to oversee the review of the Standard at appropriate intervals.

2.2 Technical Advisory Committee

Each BRC Global Standard is supported by at least one Technical Advisory Committee (TAC) who meet regularly to discuss technical, operational and interpretational issues related to the Standard. The BRC provides the technical secretariat for these groups.

The TAC is made up of senior technical managers representing the users of the Standard and includes representatives of retailers, food manufacturers, trade associations for each sector, Certification Bodies and independent technical experts.

The Standard is reviewed every three years to assess the need for updating or production of a new issue. This work is undertaken by the TAC, which is expanded for the purpose to include other available expertise.

The TAC also reviews auditor competence requirements, proposed training materials and supplementary technical documents supporting the Standards.

2.3 The Certification Body co-operation groups

The BRC encourages and facilitates meetings of the Certification Bodies participating in the scheme (co-operation groups) to discuss matters arising on the implementation of the Standard and discuss issues of interpretation. These groups report regularly to the BRC on operational issues, implementation and suggested improvements. Representatives from the co-operation groups attend the TAC meetings.

Figure 5 Governance of the BRC schemes

3   Achieving Consistency – Compliance

The maintenance of a high and consistent standard of audit and certification, and the ability of the certificated sites to maintain the standards achieved at the audit, are essential to confidence in the scheme and to the value of certification. The BRC therefore has an active compliance programme to supplement the work of accreditation bodies and ensure high standards are maintained.

The BRC scheme may only be certificated by Certification Bodies registered and approved by the BRC and accredited by a BRC-recognised accreditation body. All auditors undertaking audits against the Standard must meet the BRC auditor competency requirements and shall be registered with the BRC. All audits undertaken against the Standard shall be uploaded onto the BRC Directory, which provides the BRC with an oversight of the activity of the Certification Bodies and the opportunity to review the quality of the reports produced.

To support the Standard, the BRC operates a compliance programme which reviews the performance of the Certification Bodies, samples the quality of audit reports, assesses levels of understanding of the scheme requirements and investigates any issues or complaints. As part of this programme the BRC provides feedback on the performance of each Certification Body through a key performance indicator (KPI) programme.

On occasions, the BRC may audit the offices of Certification Bodies and accompany auditors on audits at sites to observe the performance of auditors. The BRC may also undertake independent visits to certificated sites to ensure standards of food safety and quality are being maintained in line with their certification status and ensure that the audit and reporting process is to the expected standard.

3.1   Calibrating auditors

A key component of the scheme is the calibration of the auditors to ensure a consistent understanding and application of the requirements. All Certification Bodies are required to have processes to calibrate their own auditors. An essential element of the training and calibration of auditors is the witnessed audit programme. Auditors are observed during an audit and provided with feedback on the performance of the audit. In order to ensure consistency between Certification Bodies and for the purposes of accreditation, an audit may be witnessed by a BRC representative or accreditation body auditor. Guidelines apply to these activities to ensure that sites are not disadvantaged by the presence of two auditors. This process forms an essential part of the scheme and sites are obliged to permit witnessed audits as part of the conditions for certification.

3.2   Feedback

Companies audited against the Standard may wish to provide feedback to the Certification Body or the BRC on the performance of the auditor. Such feedback sent to the BRC will be considered in confidence. Feedback provides a valuable input to the BRC monitoring programme for Certification Body performance.

3.3   Complaints and referrals

The BRC has implemented a formal complaint and referral process, which is available to organisations involved with the Global Standards. A document detailing the Global Standards referral process can be found on the website www.brcglobalstandards.com together with a 'Global Standard referral notification' form.

From time to time, failure to apply the principles and criteria of the BRC Global Standards at certificated sites may be reported to the BRC by, for example, retailers and companies conducting their own audits. In this event, the BRC will request a documented report of the reasons for the complaint and refer this report, in confidence, to the Certification Body conducting the audit. The BRC will require a full investigation of the issues raised and a report from the Certification Body submitted to the BRC within 28 calendar days (or shorter time as specified by the BRC in urgent cases).

APPENDICES

Appendix 1

The *Global Standard for Food Safety* and its Relationship with Other BRC Global Standards

The BRC has developed a range of Global Standards which set out the requirements for the manufacture of food and consumer products, the packaging used to protect the products and the storage and distribution of these products. The other BRC Standards complement the Food Safety Standard and provide a resource for the auditing and certification of suppliers.

The BRC *Global Standard for Packaging and Packaging Materials* is an auditing Standard that lays down the requirements for the manufacturing of packaging materials used for food and consumer products. Food and non-food businesses may request this from their suppliers of packaging.

The BRC *Global Standard for Storage and Distribution* is an auditing Standard that sets out the requirements for the storage, distribution, wholesaling and contracted services for packaged and un-packaged food products, packaging materials and consumer goods. The Standard is not applicable to storage facilities under the direct control of the production facility management, which is covered by the relevant manufacturing Standard (e.g. the Food Safety Standard).

The BRC *Global Standard for Consumer Products* is an auditing Standard applicable to the manufacture and assembly of consumer products. This specifically excludes food-associated products such as vitamins, minerals and herbal supplements, which fall within the scope of the BRC Global Standards for Food Safety.

Appendix 2

Guidelines on Defining Production Risk Zones

The Standard identifies four different risk zones within the processing and storage facilities, with corresponding levels of hygiene requirements and segregation to reduce the potential for product contamination. The decision tree (Figure 6) provides a guide to defining the risk zones classified as:

- Enclosed product area
- Low risk – open product area
- High care – open product area
- High risk – open product area.

The food safety controls operated within the factory areas shall be appropriate for the risks to the product. The expectations for factory hygiene, finish of the buildings, equipment and protective clothing/staff hygiene should reflect the potential risks to the product. Identifying areas of different risk helps to ensure appropriate food safety controls are in place and identify the need to restrict the movement of personnel and materials between areas.

1   Enclosed Product Area

An enclosed product area is defined as an area of the factory where all of the products are fully enclosed and therefore not vulnerable to environmental contamination (e.g. by foreign bodies or micro-organisms).

This includes areas where:

- the product is fully enclosed within packaging, e.g. raw material and finished product storage and dispatch areas
- the product is fully enclosed within equipment shielding the product from physical or microbiological contamination from the production environment *during* production. This may include enclosure within transfer pipework and fully enclosed equipment, and also where the equipment maintains its own environment to protect the product, e.g. aseptic filling equipment.

Areas meeting these criteria are typically found in liquid processing plants (e.g. dairies, wineries, and soft drinks or water bottling factories) and some highly mechanised industries such as flour mills, sugar refining and oil processing facilities.

2   Open Product Areas

Wherever ingredients, intermediate or finished products are not protected from the factory environment there is a potential risk of product contamination by foreign bodies, allergenic material or micro-organisms in the environment.

The significance of the risk of microbiological contamination will depend upon the susceptibility of the product to support the growth or survival of pathogens and the expected storage conditions, shelf life and further treatment of the product at the factory or by the consumer.

In determining the zones particular consideration shall be given to the risks presented by pathogens such as *Listeria* species). It should be recognised that some products considered as low risk on this basis will nevertheless require high standards of microbiological control, similar to a high-care area, because spoilage organisms present a significant risk (e.g. yeasts in yogurt, mould on hard cheese).

2.1   Low risk

In this area the greatest risk can be considered as physical contamination. The significance to human health of microbiological contamination is reduced because the product is unsuitable for the growth of pathogens or is designed to undergo a later validated kill step that ensures the product is safe to eat. Consideration does, however, need to be given to the risk of pre-process spoilage and of contamination by pathogens which may survive but not grow on products (e.g. salmonella on chocolate, peanut butter or dried milk powder).

The hygiene standards in such areas generally require greater emphasis on preventing foreign body and allergen contamination of products.

These areas include:

- the production of products which will always require cooking before consumption, e.g. raw meats, prepared meals and pizzas with uncooked components and where instructions require products are to be fully cooked* before eating

- production facilities where products are either processed within the final container or are unsuitable for the growth of pathogens and therefore stored and distributed as ambient products, e.g. canned products, pH-controlled products such as pickles, low a_w foods such as dried foods and confectionery, and some baked products

- production facilities where ready-to-eat products are stored chilled to preserve the quality of the product but which have other controls to prevent the growth of pathogens, e.g. hard cheese

- production areas where processes are undertaken prior to the introduction of a validated kill step in the process, such as cooking, e.g. mixing and preparation areas prior to cooking.

2.2   High care

This is an area designed to a high standard where practices relating to personnel, ingredients, equipment, packaging and environment aim to *minimise* product contamination by pathogenic micro-organisms. Segregation of the high-care area and access arrangements to the area shall minimise the risk of product contamination.

Products requiring handling in a high-care area have all of the following characteristics:

- potentially vulnerable to the growth of pathogens

- all microbiologically susceptible components have received a process to reduce the microbiological contamination to safe levels (typically 1–2 log reduction of micro-organisms) before entry to the area

- the finished products are ready to eat or heat** or, on the basis of known consumer use, are likely to be eaten without adequate cooking (see HACCP 2.3.1)

- the finished products require chilling or freezing during storage.

Although all vulnerable products have, before entry to the high-care area, received a process to reduce pathogenic bacteria to a level to make the products safe to eat, spoilage organisms will be present and shall be controlled by temperature and shelf life. Examples of products produced in such an area include sandwiches, ready prepared salads, unpasteurised soft cheeses, fermented and dried meats, cold smoked salmon, prepared meals designed to be reheated only and some chilled pizzas.

Products produced in high-care areas may themselves present hazards to other products; for instance the use of salad products, even when processed by rinsing in chlorine solution to reduce microbial load, may still present an increased risk of *Listeria*, and this needs to be taken into account when planning hygiene regimes and production planning within the high-care area.

Where a customer specifically requires their products to be produced in a high-care area, this shall not compromise the safety of other products produced in the same high-care area.

2.3   High risk

A physically segregated area, designed to a high standard of hygiene where practices relating to personnel, ingredients, equipment packaging and environment aim to prevent contamination by pathogenic micro-organisms.

Products requiring handling in a high-risk area have all of the following characteristics:

■   potentially vulnerable to the growth of pathogens, particularly *Listeria* species

■   all components have received a full cook process, minimum 70°C for 2 minutes or equivalent before entry to the area

■   the finished products are ready to eat or heat** or, on the basis of known consumer use, are likely to be eaten without adequate cooking (see HACCP 2.3.1)

■   the finished products require chilling or freezing during storage.

Products considered as high risk include cooked sliced meats, fully cooked prepared meals and dairy desserts.

Where products are designed such that they meet the requirements for a re-heat product (i.e. all components receive a full cook of 70°C for 2 minutes but also have full cooking instructions), these should be considered for production in high-risk areas.

Specific high-care and high-risk requirements

The requirements relating to processing environment and general GMPs within the Standard are always expected to be adopted in relation to product risk. There are, however, some clauses within the Standard which identify particular and specific requirements applying to high-care or high-risk areas to ensure a consistent expectation. In such clauses the words High care and High risk will appear in bold type. These clauses are 4.3.1, 4.3.5, 4.3.6, 4.4.4, 4.4.13, 4.8.4, 4.8.5 and 4.11.5.

The presence of high-care and high-risk areas and the controls in place at the site shall be included on the audit report.

Definitions

*Cook – is a thermal process undertaken by the user of the product which is designed to achieve typically a 6 log reduction in *Listeria monocytogenes* equivalent to 70°C for 2 minutes. Alternative cooking processes may be accepted where these meet recognised national guidelines and are validated by scientific data.

**Reheat – products that are designed to be safe to be consumed without the need for a full cook; the reheating of the product is intended to make the product more palatable and is not a microbiological kill step.

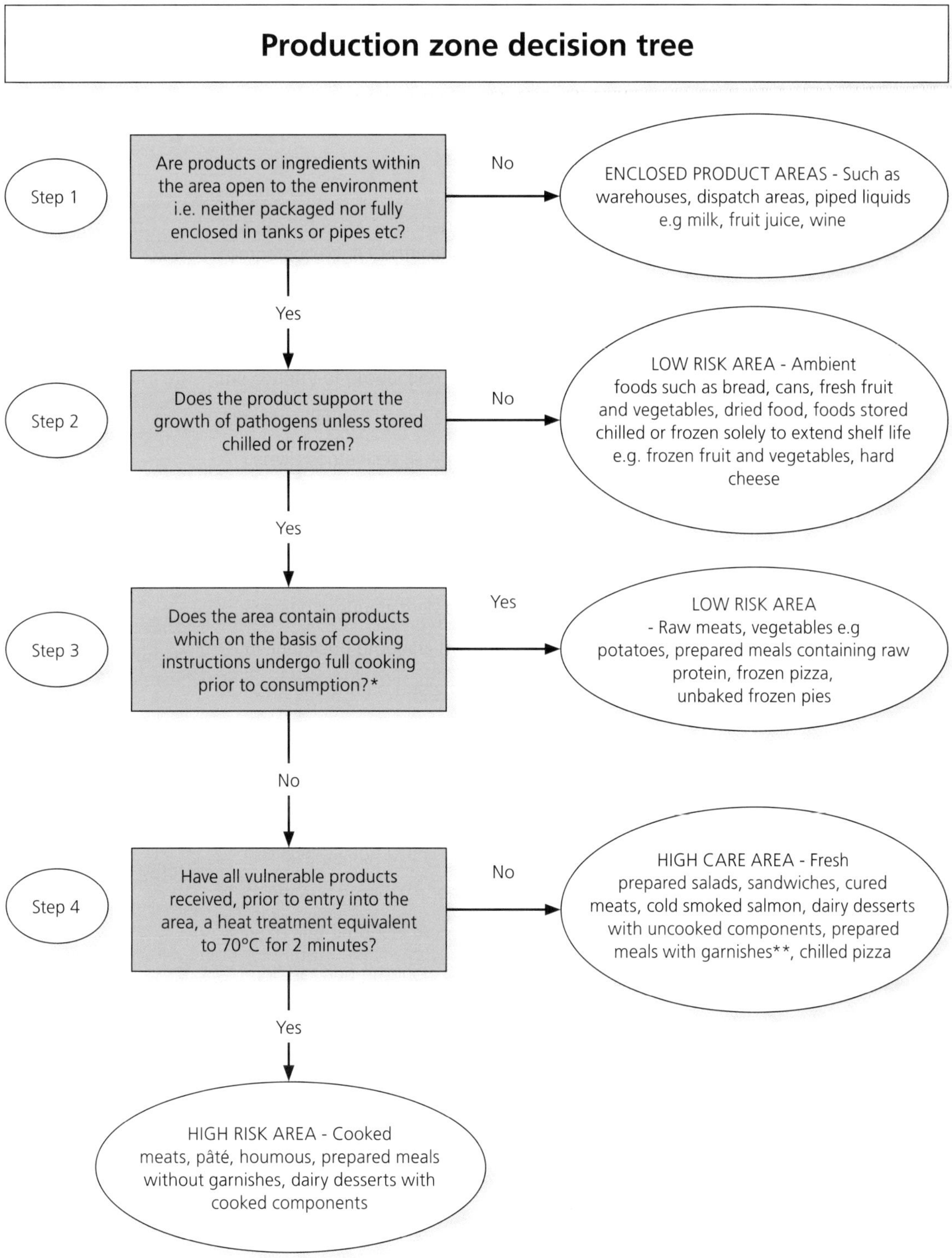

Production zone decision tree

Step 1 — Are products or ingredients within the area open to the environment i.e. neither packaged nor fully enclosed in tanks or pipes etc?

→ **No** → ENCLOSED PRODUCT AREAS - Such as warehouses, dispatch areas, piped liquids e.g milk, fruit juice, wine

↓ **Yes**

Step 2 — Does the product support the growth of pathogens unless stored chilled or frozen?

→ **No** → LOW RISK AREA - Ambient foods such as bread, cans, fresh fruit and vegetables, dried food, foods stored chilled or frozen solely to extend shelf life e.g. frozen fruit and vegetables, hard cheese

↓ **Yes**

Step 3 — Does the area contain products which on the basis of cooking instructions undergo full cooking prior to consumption?*

→ **Yes** → LOW RISK AREA - Raw meats, vegetables e.g potatoes, prepared meals containing raw protein, frozen pizza, unbaked frozen pies

↓ **No**

Step 4 — Have all vulnerable products received, prior to entry into the area, a heat treatment equivalent to 70°C for 2 minutes?

→ **No** → HIGH CARE AREA - Fresh prepared salads, sandwiches, cured meats, cold smoked salmon, dairy desserts with uncooked components, prepared meals with garnishes**, chilled pizza

↓ **Yes**

HIGH RISK AREA - Cooked meats, pâté, houmous, prepared meals without garnishes, dairy desserts with cooked components

* Thermal treatment equivalent to 70°C for 2 minutes.
** Raw or not pH/a_w stabilised so will support the growth of *L.monocytogenes*.

Figure 6 Production zone decision tree

This decision tree provides a guide only to the categorisation of production zones and cannot take account of specific product characteristics (e.g. pH, a_w) or the vulnerability of particular products to pathogens or spoilage which may result in exceptions. A detailed risk assessment should be undertaken where necessary to support the decision. Reference shall be made to the more detailed explanations of product zones in the guideline.

Appendix 3

Qualifications, Training and Experience Requirements for Auditors

The following identify the minimum requirements for auditors to conduct audits against the BRC *Global Standard for Food Safety*.

Education

The auditor shall have a degree in a food-related or bioscience discipline, or as a minimum have successfully completed a higher education course in a food or bioscience-related discipline.

Work Experience

The auditor shall have a minimum of five years' post-qualification experience related to the food industry. This shall involve work in quality assurance or food safety functions within manufacturing, retailing, inspection or enforcement, and the auditor shall be able to demonstrate an understanding and knowledge of specific product categories for which they are approved. The verification of the auditor's ability to carry out work within specific product categories is the responsibility of the Certification Body.

Qualifications

The auditor must have:

- passed a registered Management System Lead Assessor Course (e.g. IRCA) or the BRC Third Party Auditor course delivered by a BRC approved trainer.

- completed a training course in HACCP (as evidenced by examination), based on the principles of Codex Alimentarius, of at least two days' duration, and be able to demonstrate competence in the understanding and application of HACCP principles. It is essential that the HACCP course is recognised by the industry (and its stakeholders) as being appropriate and relevant.

Audit Training

Auditors must have successfully completed a period of supervised training (including witnessed audits) in practical assessment through 10 audits or 15 audit days involving third-party food safety audits against Global Food Safety Initiative (GFSI) approved Standards, ISO 22000 or ISO 9000 series (at a food company) of which at least five audits must be against the *Global Standard for Food Safety*.

Certification Bodies must be able to demonstrate that every auditor has appropriate training and experience for the particular categories for which they are considered competent. Auditor competence shall be recorded at least at the level of each category, as indicated in Appendix 4.

Certification Bodies must establish training programmes for each auditor that incorporate:

- a *Global Standard for Food Safety* awareness course delivered by a BRC approved trainer

- a period of initial training covering product safety, HACCP and prerequisite programmes, and access to relevant laws and regulations

- a period of supervised training to cover quality management systems, audit techniques and specific category knowledge

- assessment of knowledge and skills for each category
- documented sign-off after the satisfactory completion of the training programme.

Each auditor's training programme shall be managed and approved by a technically competent person within the Certification Body who can demonstrate technical competence in the categories in which training is given.

Full detailed training records of the individual shall be maintained by the Certification Body throughout the term of employment, and retained for a minimum period of five years after leaving the employment of the Certification Body.

Exceptions

Where a Certification Body employs an auditor who does not fully meet the specific criteria for education but has been assessed as competent, there shall be a fully documented justification in place to support the employment of the auditor.

Note – such exceptions only apply to existing auditors.

Responsibility of the Certification Body

It is the responsibility of the Certification Body to ensure processes are in place to monitor and maintain the competence of the auditor to the level required by the Standard.

Appendix 4

Product Categories

The following product examples are given as guidance only and this is not an exhaustive list. The BRC will publish updated examples on the BRC website www.brcglobalstandards.com

Field of audit	Category no.	Category description	Product examples	Storage conditions	Examples of knowledge of technology required by auditor
Raw products of animal or vegetable origin that require cooking prior to consumption	1	Raw red meat	Beef/veal, pork, lamb, venison, offal, other meat	Chilled Frozen	Slaughter, primary cutting Vacuum packing Modified atmosphere packaging
	2	Raw poultry	Chicken, turkey, duck, goose, quail, farmed and wild game Shell egg	Chilled Frozen	Slaughter and primary cutting Vacuum packing Modified atmosphere packaging
	3	Raw prepared products (meat, fish and vegetarian)	Bacon, comminuted meat products (e.g. sausages), meat puddings, ready-to-cook meals, ready prepared meat products, pizzas, vegetable prepared meals, steamer meals, comminuted fish products (e.g. fish fingers)	Chilled Frozen	Butchery, processing and packing Curing, vacuum packing, modified atmosphere packaging
	4	Raw fish products and preparations	Wet fish, molluscs, crustacea, cold smoked fish, ready prepared fish products	Chilled Frozen	Stunning, harvesting Vacuum packing, modified atmosphere packaging

Field of audit	Category no.	Category description	Product examples	Storage conditions	Examples of knowledge of technology required by auditor
Fruit, vegetables and nuts	5	Fruit, vegetables and nuts	Fruit, vegetables, salads, herbs, nuts (unroasted)	Fresh	Washing, grading
	6	Prepared fruit, vegetables and nuts	Prepared/semi-processed fruit, vegetables and salads including prepared ready-to-eat salads, coleslaws, chips, frozen vegetables	Chilled Frozen	Blanching, freezing High-care principles
Processed foods and liquids with pasteurisation or UHT as heat treatment or similar technology	7	Dairy, liquid egg	Liquid egg, liquid milk/drinks, cream, liquid tea and coffee creamers, yogurts, fermented milk-based products, fromage frais/crème fraîche, butter	Chilled Frozen	Dairy technology – pasteurisation, separation, fermentation High-risk principles
			Ice cream	Frozen	
			Cheeses – hard, soft, mould ripened, unpasteurised, processed, cheese food	Chilled	
			Long-life milks, non-dairy products (e.g. soya milk), ambient yogurts, custards, etc.	Ambient	
			Fruit juices (includes freshly squeezed and pasteurised, smoothies)	Chilled Ambient	
			Dried whey powder, dried egg, dried milk/milk formulation	Ambient	

Field of audit	Category no.	Category description	Product examples	Storage conditions	Examples of knowledge of technology required by auditor
Processed foods Ready-to-eat or heat and eat foods, i.e. heat treatment or segregation and processes that control product safety	8	Cooked meat/ fish products	Cooked meats (e.g. ham, meat pâté, molluscs (ready to eat), crustaceans (ready to eat), fish pâté) Hot smoked fish, poached salmon	Chilled Frozen	High care/risk principles Vacuum packs Heat treatment
	9	Raw cured and/or fermented meat and fish	Parma ham, cold smoked salmon (e.g. gravlax), air-dried meats/ salami, ready-to-eat smoked fish, fermented meats, dried fish	Chilled	Curing, fermentation High care/risk principles
	10	Ready meals and sandwiches; ready-to-eat desserts	Ready meals, sandwiches, soups, sauces, pasta, quiche, flans, meal accompaniments, cream cakes, trifles, assembled high-risk sweet desserts, hot eating pies, cold eating pies	Chilled Frozen	High care/risk principles
Ambient stable products with pasteurisation or sterilisation as heat treatment	11	Low/high acid in cans/glass	Canned products (e.g. beans, soups, meals, fruit, tuna) Products packed in glass (e.g. sauces, jams, pickled vegetables) Pet food	Ambient	Canning Thermal processing UHT

Field of audit	Category no.	Category description	Product examples	Storage conditions	Examples of knowledge of technology required by auditor
Ambient stable products not involving sterilisation as heat treatment	12	Beverages	Soft drinks including flavoured water, isotonics, concentrates, squashes, cordials, minerals, table waters, ice, herbal drinks, food drinks	Ambient	Water treatment Heat treatment
	13	Alcoholic drinks and fermented/ brewed products	Beer, wine, spirits Vinegars Alcopops	Ambient	Distilling, fermentation, fortification
	14	Bakery	Bread, pastry, biscuits, cakes, tarts, breadcrumbs	Ambient Frozen	Baking
	15	Dried foods and ingredients	Soups, sauces, gravies, spices, stocks, herbs, seasonings, stuffings, pulses, legumes, rice, noodles, nut preparations, fruit preparations, dried pet food, vitamins, salt, additives, gelatine, glacé fruit, home baking, syrups, sugar, flour Tea, instant coffee and coffee creamers	Ambient	Drying Heat treatment
	16	Confectionery	Chocolate, gums and jellies, other sweets	Ambient	Heat treatment
	17	Breakfast cereals and snacks	Porridge oats, muesli, breakfast cereals, roasted nuts, crisps, poppadoms	Ambient	Extrusion, heat treatment

Field of audit	Category no.	Category description	Product examples	Storage conditions	Examples of knowledge of technology required by auditor
	18	Oils and fats	Cooking oils, margarine, shortening, spreads, suet, ghee Salad dressings, mayonnaise, vinaigrettes	Ambient	Refining, hydrogenation

Appendix 5

Certificate Template

CERTIFICATION BODY NAME OR LOGO

Auditor number
_____

This is to certify that
COMPANY NAME
BRC site code
AUDIT SITE ADDRESS

Has been evaluated by Certification Body name (a national accreditation body) accredited Certification Body No. X and found to meet the requirements of

Global Standard for Food Safety
ISSUE 6: JULY 2011

SCOPE

Exclusions from Scope
Product Categories

Achieved Grade

Audit programme: (i.e. Announced, Unannounced Option 1 or Option 2, reissued after extension to scope)

Date(s) of audit: include two date ranges for unannounced option 2, if an extension to scope include original audit date and visit date

Certificate issue date:

Re-audit due date: from   to

Certificate expiry date:

_____

Authorised by

Accreditation body logo	**Name and full address of Certification Body** Certificate traceability reference This certificate remains the property of (name of Certification Body)	BRC logo

Appendix 6

Certificate Validity, Audit Frequency and Planning

Example of Announced audit 6 or 12 months' certificate validity

Audit	Event	Date	Explanation
Initial audit (audit 1)	Initial audit date	1 February 2012	
	Certificate issue date	12 March 2012	The company takes 28 days to submit all corrective actions The Certification Body takes 12 days to issue the certificate (14 days allowed)
	Certificate expiry date	14 March 2013	Anniversary of the initial audit date plus 42 days
	Re-audit due date	4 January to 1 February 2013	12 months from the (first day) initial audit including 28-day audit window
Re-certification audit (audit 2)	Actual re-audit visit	26 January 2013	Company is allowed a 28-day window before the audit due date
	Certificate issue date	25 February 2013	The company takes 20 days to submit all corrective actions (28 days allowed) The Certification Body takes 10 days to issue the certificate (14 days allowed)
	Certificate expiry date	14 September 2013 or 14 March 2014	This is 6 or 12 months plus 42 days from the initial audit date. This allows the site to take the audit up to 28 days early without losing time from the certificate
	Recertification audit due date	4 July to 1 August 2013 or 4 January to 1 February 2014	18 months from the (first day) initial audit including 28-day audit window 24 months from the (first day) initial audit including 28-day audit window

Example following audits to Unannounced scheme option 1

Audit	Event	Date	Explanation
Audit 1	Announced audit	1 January 2012	
	Certificate expiry date	12 February 2013	12-month anniversary of (initial) audit plus 42 days
	Re-audit due date	4 December 2012 to 1 January 2013	12 months from the first day of initial audit including 28-day audit window
Audit 2 Unannounced completed 1 Oct 2012	Site opts into unannounced audit option 1	By 1 April 2012	Within 3 months of announced audit, assuming site achieves A or B grade*
	Unannounced re-audit will take place	Between 1 April 2012 and 1 January 2013	Audit occurs between 3 and 12 months after announced audit
	Certificate issue date	31 October 2012	The company takes 20 days to submit all corrective actions (28 days allowed. The Certification Body takes 10 days to issue the certificate (14 days allowed) Certificate supersedes any current certificate
	Certificate expiry date	12 February 2014	24-month anniversary of (initial) audit plus 42 days if remaining in unannounced scheme
	Re-audit due date on certificate	Between 1 April 2013 and 1 January 2014	24 months from the first day of initial audit including 28-day audit window. Assuming the site remains in the unannounced programme
Audit 3	Site remains in unannounced scheme option 1	Confirms choice by 1 April 2013	
	Unannounced audit due between	Between 1 April 2013 and 1 January 2014	The audit window is within 3 and 12 months of the initial announced audit, not the previous audit
Audit 3 Site reverts to Announced scheme by choice (grade A+ or B+) – or due to resulting grade C+	Re-audit due date	3 September to 1 October 2013 or 4 March 2013 to 1 April 2013	Now reverts back to 6- or 12-month anniversary of last unannounced audit date including 28-day audit window
	Certificate expiry date	13 November 2013 or 13 May 2013	Audit due date anniversary (6 or 12 months) plus 42 days

Audit	Event	Date	Explanation
Audit 3	Site opts into unannounced audit option 2	By 1 April 2013	
	Re-audit GMP (part 1) unannounced due date	1 July 2013 to 1 November 2013	Audit occurs between 6 and 10 months of audit cycle
	Re-audit management systems (part 2) announced due date	Between 4 December 2013 and 1 January 2014	Anniversary of initial audit date within 28-day window
	Certificate expiry date	12 February 2014	Audit due date anniversary plus 42 days

Example following audits to Unannounced scheme option 2.

Audit	Event	Date	Explanation
Audit 1	Announced audit	1 January 2012	
	Certificate issue date	12 February 2012	
	Certificate expiry date	12 February 2013	12-month anniversary of (initial) audit plus 42 days
	Re-audit due date	4 December 2012 to 1 January 2013	12 months from the first day of initial audit including 28-day audit window
	Site opts into unannounced audit option 2	By 1 April 2012	Within 3 months of announced audit, assuming site achieves A or B grade*
Audit 2 23 September 2012	Re-audit GMP (part 1) unannounced due date	1 June 2012 to 1 November 2012	Audit occurs between 6 and 10 months after last announced audit
	Re-audit management systems (part 2) announced due date	Between 4 December 2012 and 1 January 2013	Anniversary of initial audit date within 28-day window
	Certificate expiry date	12 February 2013	Audit due date anniversary plus 42 days

Audit	Event	Date	Explanation
Audit 3	Site chooses to stay in unannounced option 2	Confirm by 1 April 2013	
	Re-audit GMP (part 1) unannounced due date	1 June 2013 to 1 November 2013	Audit occurs between 6 and 10 months of audit cycle
	Re-audit management systems (part 2) announced due date	Between 4 December 2013 and 1 January 2014	Anniversary of initial audit date within 28-day window
	Certificate expiry date	12 February 2014	Audit due date anniversary plus 42 days

All sites must have an initial 'announced audit' before moving to an unannounced scheme.

*Only sites which achieve an 'A' or 'B' grade may continue to take part in the unannounced audit scheme.

Appendix 7

Audit of Multiple Sites

The scope of a BRC audit needs to be agreed between the site and the Certification Body prior to the audit.

The audit, report and certificate shall be 'product' and 'site' specific. However, in some circumstances, more than one site may be included under a single certification. This will be considered exceptional, but allowable under the following rules.

Audits may cover multiple site addresses where ALL of the following rules apply:

- all sites are under the same organisation ownership
- all sites are operated against the same documented quality management systems
- sites manufacture product which is part of the same manufacturing process
- the sites solely supply the other sites with no additional customers
- the sites are no more than 30 miles/50 km apart.

All sites must be visited as part of the same audit schedule (i.e. within same timeframe).

The Certification Body's audit plan needs to clearly show the sites that shall be audited.

It must be clearly stated on the report and certificate that the audit has consisted of visits to more than one site address (e.g. the manufacture of cheese at Cheddar Industrial Estate, Wensleydale, Yorkshire and maturation at Camembert Road, Ripon).

Auditing of Activities Managed by a Group or Head Office Located Separately from the Manufacturing Site

When undertaking audits of sites which are part of a larger manufacturing group, it is not uncommon for some of the requirements within the scope of the Standard to be undertaken by a central or head office. Typically this may apply to activities such as purchasing, supplier approval, product development, product recall and, occasionally, this extends to a group shared quality management system – document control and procedures.

All requirements within the scope of the Standard must be assessed as satisfactory before a certificate can be issued. This requires that any centrally managed systems are included within the audit process; however, there are alternative processes for achieving this.

There are two approaches to auditing the requirements which are managed at a central office:

1 Request and review information whilst at the manufacturing site as part of the site audit – Standard audit.

2 Undertake a separate audit of the centrally managed processes at the group/head office location – Two-stage audit.

1   Approach 1 – Requesting and reviewing information at the manufacturing site

Recommended only where:

- satisfactory links can be established with the central office –
  - telephone or video conference to allow interview of relevant personnel
  - fax, email links to allow documents to be requested and viewed

- arrangements are in place to ensure availability of relevant personnel
- the amount and type of information can be effectively reviewed and challenged remotely.

Note – Where a site elects for the information to be assessed during the manufacturing site audit and satisfactory information cannot be provided during the audit, unsubstantiated requirements shall be recorded as non-conformities on the site audit report.

1.1   Reporting

The audit report shall make it clear where a requirement is managed by a central office together with a comment on how the company complies with the requirement.

1.2   Non-conformities

Non-conformities raised against a centrally operated requirement shall be recorded on the audit report and included within the count of non-conformities contributing to the site grade.

Corrective action shall be assessed in the same way as for non-conformities raised at the manufacturing site and must be satisfactorily corrected before a certificate can be issued to the site.

1.3   Subsequent manufacturing-site audits

The central systems requirements shall be challenged and evidence of compliance be provided at each manufacturing site audit.

2   Approach 2 – Two-stage audits: central systems and separate manufacturing-site audit

This approach is recommended where it is not practical to effectively assess requirements from the manufacturing site. For example, where:

- practical arrangements to allow assessment cannot be provided
- there are too many centrally managed requirements to effectively review remotely.

This shall be offered to the company being audited and undertaken when requested by the company.

2.1   Stage 1 – Central system audit

The audit of the central systems shall be completed before undertaking the manufacturing site audit.

The audit shall assess both how the central system complies with the relevant requirement of the Standard and how this links to the manufacturing site operation.

2.1.1   Reports for the central system audit

The Certification Body may produce a report of the central system audit for the benefit of the company; however, as this audit will only include some of the requirements of the BRC standard:

- no grade may be allocated
- no certificate may be issued
- the report must be in a format which is clearly different from the full BRC audit report.

The central system report shall not be uploaded to the BRC Directory but the findings of the central system audit shall be incorporated into the final audit report of each of the associated manufacturing sites.

2.1.2   Recording non-conformities identified at the central system audit

All non-conformities identified at the central office audit shall be recorded on the audit report of the first manufacturing site audited following the central systems audit – irrespective of whether these have been closed out before that audit or not.

However, only those non-conformities raised at the central office audit which have not been closed out to the satisfaction of the Certification Body at the time of the manufacturing site audit shall be counted when calculating the grade for the manufacturing site.

Any non-conformities identified at the head office audit which are still outstanding at the time of further manufacturing site audits (2nd, 3rd etc.) shall be included on that manufacturing site report and be included when calculating the grade for the site. (See worked example Appendix 1).

2.1.3   Closure of central systems corrective actions

Corrective actions required following the central office audit shall be assessed in the same way as corrective actions raised at the manufacturing site and must be satisfactorily corrected before a certificate can be issued to the manufacturing sites. This may be by documentary evidence or a revisit, as appropriate.

2.2   Stage 2 – Audits of the manufacturing site(s)

Information from the central office audit (including any evidence of corrective actions taken) shall be made available to the auditors of the associated manufacturing sites by the Certification Body.

The auditor shall establish that the central systems components assessed are the same as those operating at the manufacturing site. The auditor shall verify any corrective actions already taken following the central systems audit.

2.2.1   Audit duration

It may be possible to reduce the duration of the manufacturing site audit to take account of systems already audited at a central office.

2.2.2   BRC audit report

The final audit report shall be applicable to the manufacturing site.

The central office audit shall be commented upon in the Company Profile; for example: 'An audit was carried out at the central office at .... on .... to assess requirements as indicated in the report'.

The Key Personnel may include the names of key staff present at the central office audit.

The manufacturing site(s) audit report shall include information about how both the site and the central system comply with the requirements of the Standard. The report shall indicate where a requirement is managed by a central office and provide an explanation of how that requirement is satisfied.

2.2.3   Corrective action

The 28 days allowed for evidence of corrective action to be provided starts from the date of the manufacturing site audit.

It is the responsibility of the site to ensure that head office corrective actions have been provided to the Certification Body in order to allow the site to become certificated. This will require effective communication with the central systems office.

Where central systems corrective actions have been accepted prior to the first manufacturing site audit, this shall be indicated on the first manufacturing site audit report and the date of acceptance of the action indicated in the 'action taken' section of the non-compliance report.

2.2.4   Certificate

The certificate, where awarded, is issued to the manufacturing site. The re-audit date for the manufacturing site is based on the grade achieved and shall be 6 or 12 months from the initial audit date.

The central office audits shall be carried out every 12 months and shall occur before the anniversary of the audit of the first manufacturing site.

2.2.5   Audits of other manufacturing sites associated with the central system

Usually there will be several manufacturing sites associated with a central system. The information from the annual central system audit shall be used for each subsequent manufacturing site audit.

Non-conformities originally raised at the central office and effectively corrected before the audit of that manufacturing site shall not be recorded as non-conformities on the site audit report. Any outstanding non-conformities at the time of the manufacturing site audit shall, however, be included within that site's report and calculation for grading purposes.

The BRC shall be contacted for advice before carrying out audit programmes for more complex arrangements of sites and centralised systems; contact brcglobalstandards@brc.org.uk

Appendix 8

Extension to Scope

Once certification has been granted, any additional significant products manufactured or processes undertaken by the site, which are required to be included in the scope of certification, must be communicated to the Certification Body. The Certification Body shall assess the significance of the new products or processes and decide whether to conduct a site visit to examine the aspects of the required extension to scope.

A revisit is required before granting a scope extension in the following circumstances:

- inclusion of manufacturing facilities not taken into account in the original audit

- inclusion of a new processing technology, e.g. canning of low-acid products where formerly only high-acid products were within scope

- inclusion of new products which introduce a significant new risk to the facility, e.g. addition of a nut-based product to a previously allergen-free site.

A revisit is less likely where:

- new products are extensions to the existing ranges produced on existing equipment.

Where an extension to scope is required shortly before the certificate is due to expire, it may be more appropriate to undertake a full audit and issue a new certificate. This option should be agreed between the Certification Body and their client prior to undertaking the extension to scope audit.

When a revisit is considered necessary, the duration of this visit will vary depending on the aspects to be examined for the required extension to scope. The site visit should be conducted along the same principles as the original audit (i.e. including an opening meeting, inspection of the operation of the process, documentation trails and closing meeting). The revisit should be announced, irrespective of whether the site is certificated to the announced or unannounced scheme.

Identified non-conformities should be documented and actioned within the normal protocol of the Standard (i.e. the company has 28 days to provide appropriate evidence of close out and the Certification Body should review the information and confirm the certification decision in the normal manner). The additional non-conformities raised at the site visit will affect neither the current certificated grade nor continued certification. However, if practices are seen that give the Certification Body cause to doubt continued certification (e.g. the identification of a critical non-conformity) then the Certification Body shall arrange a full re-audit of the site. In these circumstances the current certificate shall be withdrawn.

A visit report should be documented, but shall not be in the format of a standard BRC audit report. A short explanation of the nature of the visit, what was audited and the conclusions should be given. The visit report should document what controls are in place and confirm the effectiveness of these controls. It should be clear in the report what aspects were looked at and what was excluded.

The site's current certificate will be superseded by any new certificate issued. The certificate must use the same expiry date as detailed on the original certificate. The due date of the next full audit will therefore remain the same and this should be made clear to the supplier by the Certification Body when arranging extension to scope visits. The grade shall also remain the same.

The certificate should include identification that it was a scope extension and the date of the visit.

Appendix 9

Glossary

Accreditation	The procedure by which an authoritative body gives formal recognition of the competence of a Certification Body to provide certification services against a specified Standard.
Allergen	A known component of food which causes physiological reactions due to an immunological response (e.g. nuts and others identified in legislation relevant to the country of production or sale).

Allergens defined by the EU are:

- cereals containing gluten (wheat, rye, barley, oats, spelt, kamut or their hybridised strains) and products thereof

- crustaceans and products thereof

- eggs and products thereof

- fish and products thereof

- peanuts and products thereof

- soybeans and products thereof

- milk and products thereof

- nuts: almond (*Amygdalus communis* L), hazelnut (*Corylus avellana*), walnut (*Juglans regia*), cashew (*Anacardium occidentale*), pecan (*Carya illinoinesis* (Wangenh.) K Koch), brazil (*Bertholletia excelsa*), pistachio (*Pistacia vera*), macadamia and Queensland (*Macadamia ternifolia*) and products thereof

- celery and products thereof

- lupin and products thereof

- molluscs and products thereof

- mustard and products thereof

- sesame seeds and products thereof

- sulphur dioxide and sulphites at concentrations of more than 10 mg/kg or 10 mg/litre expressed as SO_2.

Announced audit	An audit where the company agrees the scheduled audit date in advance with the Certification Body.
Assured status	Products produced in accordance with a recognised product certification scheme, the status of which needs to be preserved through the BRC certified production facility (e.g. GlobalGAP).
ATP bioluminescence techniques	A rapid test for cleanliness of surfaces based on ATP (adenosine triphosphate) – a substance used in energy transfer in cells and therefore present in biological material.
Audit	A systematic examination to substantiate whether activities and related results comply with planned arrangements and whether these arrangements are implemented effectively and are suitable to achieve objectives.
Branded food products	Pre-packaged food products bearing the logo, copyright and address of a company which is not a retailer.

Business continuity	A framework which enables an organisation to plan and respond to incidents of business interruption in order to continue business operations at an acceptable predetermined level.
Calibration	A set of operations that establish, under specified conditions, the relationship between values of quantities indicated by a measuring instrument or measuring system, or values represented by a material measure or reference material, and the corresponding values realised by standards.
Certificate withdrawal	Where certification is revoked.
Certification	The procedure by which an accredited Certification Body, based on an audit and assessment of a company's competence, provide written assurance that a company conforms to a Standard's requirement.
Certification Body	A provider of certification services, accredited to do so by an authoritative body.
Cleaning in place (CIP)	The process of cleaning and sanitising food processing equipment in its assembled position without the need for dismantling and cleaning the individual parts.
Codex Alimentarius	The body responsible for establishing internationally recognised standards, codes of practice and guidelines, of which *HACCP* is one such standard.
Cook	A thermal process designed to heat a food item to a minimum of 70°C for 2 minutes or equivalent.
Company	The person, firm, company or other entity with whom a confirmed purchase order is placed, or who owns premises where products in whatever form originate, or who is otherwise responsible for employing or procuring the services of food handlers in the production and preparation of food.
Competence	Demonstrable ability to apply skill, knowledge and understanding of a task or subject to achieve intended results.
Contamination	Introduction or occurrence of an unwanted organism, taint or substance in food or the food environment. Types of contamination include physical, chemical, biological and allergenic. Contamination can also mean incorrect mixing of packages.
Control measure	Any action or activity that can be used to prevent or eliminate a food safety hazard or reduce it to an acceptable level.
Corrective action	Action to eliminate the cause of a detected non-conformity deviation.
Critical control point (CCP)	A step at which control can be applied and is essential to prevent or eliminate a food safety hazard or reduce it to an acceptable level.
Customer	A business or person to whom a product has been provided, either as a finished product or as a component part of the finished product.
Customer focus	A structured approach to determining and addressing the needs of an organisation to which the company supplies products and which may be measured by the use of performance indicators.
End consumer	The ultimate consumer of a foodstuff who will not use the food as part of any food business operation or activity.
Enrolment scheme	Registration is followed by an audit giving a scored result which can be used as part of a continual development plan by a company.
Factored goods	Goods not manufactured or part processed on site but bought in and sold on.
Flow diagram	A systematic representation of the sequence of steps or operations used in the production or manufacture of a particular food item.
Food handler	Anyone who handles or prepares food, whether open (unwrapped) or packaged.

Food safety	Assurance that food will not cause harm to the consumer when it is prepared and/or eaten according to its intended use.
Fundamental requirement	A requirement of the Standard that relates to a system which must be well established, continuously maintained and monitored by the company as absence or poor adherence to the system will have serious repercussions on the integrity or safety of the product supplied.
Genetically Modified Organism (GMO)	An organism whose genetic material has been altered by the techniques of genetic modification so that its DNA contains genes not normally found there.
Global Food Safety Initiative (GFSI)	Managed by the Consumer Goods Forum, a project to harmonise and benchmark international food safety standards. www.mygfsi.com
Good manufacturing practice (GMP)	Implemented procedures and practices undertaken using best practice principles
Hazard	A biological, chemical, physical or allergenic agent in food, or a condition of food, that has the potential to cause an adverse health effect.
Hazard Analysis and Critical Control Point (HACCP)	A system that identifies, evaluates and controls hazards which are significant for food safety.
High-care area	An area designed to a high standard where practices relating to personnel, ingredients, equipment, packaging and environment aim to minimise product contamination by pathogenic micro-organisms.
High-care product	A product that requires chilling or freezing during storage, is vulnerable to the growth of pathogens, received a process to reduce the microbiological contamination to safe levels (typically 1–2 log reduction) and is ready to eat or heat.
High-risk area	A physically segregated area, designed to a high standard of hygiene, where practices relating to personnel, ingredients, equipment, packaging and environment aim to prevent product contamination by pathogenic micro-organisms.
High-risk product	A chilled ready-to-eat/heat product or food where there is a high risk of growth of pathogenic micro-organisms.
Identity preserved	A product which has a defined origin or purity characteristic which needs to be retained throughout the food chain (e.g. through traceability and protection from contamination).
Incident	An event that has occurred which results in the production or supply of unsafe, illegal or non-conforming product.
Initial audit	The first BRC audit at a company/site.
Internal audit	The general process of audit, for all the activity of the company. Conducted by or on behalf of the company for internal purposes.
Job description	A list of the responsibilities for a given position at a company.
Low-risk area	An area where the processing or handling of foods presents minimum risk of product contamination or growth of micro-organisms, or where the subsequent processing or preparation of the product by the consumer will ensure product safety.
Non-conformity	The non-fulfilment of a specified product safety, legal or quality requirement or a specified system requirement.

Performance indicators	Summaries of quantified data that provide information on the level of compliance against agreed targets (e.g. customer complaints, product incidents, laboratory data).
Potable water	Water being safe to drink, free from pollutants and harmful organisms and conforming to local legal requirements.
Preparation of primary product	A food product which has undergone a washing, trimming, size-grading or quality-grading process and is pre-packed.
Prerequisite	The basic environmental and operational conditions in a food business that are necessary for the production of safe food. These control generic hazards covering *good manufacturing practice* and good hygienic practice and shall be considered within the *HACCP* study.
Primary packaging	Packaging which is in direct contact with food.
Procedure	An agreed method of carrying out an activity or process which is implemented and documented in the form of detailed instructions or process description (e.g. a flowchart).
Processed food	A food product which has undergone any of the following processes: aseptic filling, baking, battering, blending, bottling, breading, brewing, canning, coating, cooking, curing, cutting, dicing, distillation, drying, extrusion, fermentation, freeze drying, freezing, frying, hot filling, irradiation, microfiltration, microwaving, milling, mixing, being packed in modified atmosphere, being packed in vacuum packing, packing, pasteurisation, pickling, roasting, slicing, smoking, steaming or sterilisation.
Processing aid	Any substance not consumed as a food by itself, intentionally used in the processing of raw materials, foods or their ingredients to fulfil a certain technological purpose during treatment or processing, and which may result in the unintentional but technically unavoidable presence of the residues of the substance or its derivatives in the final product – provided that these residues do not present any health risk and do not have any technological effect on the finished product.
Product recall	Any measures aimed at achieving the return of an unfit product from customers and final consumers.
Product withdrawal	Any measures aimed at achieving the return of an unfit product from customers but not final consumers.
Provenance	The origin or the source of food or raw materials.
Quantity check/ mass balance	A reconciliation of the amount of incoming raw material against the amount used in the resulting finished products, also taking into account process waste and rework.
Ready-to-cook food	Food designed by the manufacturer as requiring cooking or other processing effective to eliminate or reduce to an acceptable level micro-organisms of concern.
Ready-to-eat food	Food intended by the manufacturer for direct human consumption without the need for cooking or other processing, effective to eliminate or reduce to an acceptable level micro-organisms of concern.
Ready-to-reheat food	Food designed by the manufacturer as suitable for direct human consumption without the need for cooking, but which may benefit in organoleptic quality from some warming prior to consumption.
Recognised laboratory accreditation	Laboratory accreditation schemes that have gained national and international acceptance awarded by a competent body and recognised by government bodies or users of the *Standard* (e.g. ISO 17025 or equivalents).
Retail brand	A trademark, logo, copyright or address of a retailer.
Retailer	A business selling food to the public by retail.

Retailer-branded food products	Food products bearing a retailer's logo, copyright or address; ingredients used for manufacture within a retailer's premises; or products that are legally regarded as the responsibility of the retailer.
Risk analysis	A process consisting of three components: risk assessment, risk management and risk communication.
Risk assessment	The identification, evaluation and estimation of the levels of risk involved in a process to determine an appropriate control process.
Root cause	The underlying cause of a problem which, if adequately addressed, will prevent a recurrence of that problem.
Seasonal production sites	A product harvested and processed on a site that is opened specifically for the duration of the short term of that harvest (typically 12 weeks or less) during a 12-month cycle.
Shall	Signifies a requirement to comply with the contents of the clause.
Should	Signifies the expected or desired requirement to comply with the contents of the clause.
Site	A unit of the company.
Standard, the	The BRC *Global Standard for Food Safety*, Issue 6, July 2011.
Stock reconciliation	The process by which the location and quantity of raw material, intermediate and finished product is identified and matched to product schedules and quantities.
Supplier	The person, firm, company or other entity to whom a company's purchase order to supply is addressed.
Suspension	Where certification is revoked for a given period pending remedial action on the part of the company.
Traceability	The ability to trace and follow a food, feed, food-producing animal or raw material that is intended to be, or expected to be, incorporated into a food, through all stages of receipt, production, processing and distribution.
Trend	An identified pattern of results.
Unannounced audit	An audit undertaken on a date unknown in advance to the company. There are two options provided by the *Standard*.
User	The person or organisation who requests information from the company regarding certification.
Utilities	A commodity or service, such as electricity or water, that is provided by a public body.
Validation	Confirmation through the provision of objective evidence that the requirements for the specific intended use or application have been fulfilled.
Verification	Confirmation through the provision of objective evidence that specified requirements have been fulfilled.
Where appropriate	In relation to a requirement of the Standard, the company will assess the need for the requirement and where applicable put in place systems, processes, procedures or equipment to meet the requirement. The company shall be mindful of legal requirements, best practice standards, GMP and industry guidance, and any other information relating to the manufacture of safe and legal product.

Appendix 10

Acknowledgements

The British Retail Consortium is grateful to the members of the Working Group who prepared this document:

Geoff Austin	Geoff Austin Associates Limited	**Andrew Kerridge**	Burger King
Karen Betts	British Retail Consortium	**Ron Kill**	Micron2 Ltd
Alan Botham	Northern Foods	**Phillip Knight**	Knight International Inspectorate
Paula Boult	SGS United Kingdom Ltd		
David Brackston	British Retail Consortium	**Jon Kukoly**	British Retail Consortium
Andy Brown	Food and Drink Federation	**Rob Nugent**	Provision Trade Federation
Stefano Cardinali	DNV	**Clive Manvell**	NSF-CMi Certfication Ltd
Adam Chappell	SAI Global Assurance Services Ltd	**Per Noerregaard**	Bureau Veritas
		Thomas Owen	British Retail Consortium
Roger Conen	UKAS	**Jon Revell**	EXOVA
Rachel Crocker	Campden BRI	**Linda Riley**	Independent Consultant
Derek Croucher	Morning Foods	**Geoff Spriegel**	Food Consulting Int.
Barry Eschbach	Land O Lakes	**Jon Tugwell**	Fresh Produce Consortium
Suzanne Finstad	Tyson Foods, Inc.	**Trish Twohig**	Iceland Foods Ltd
Alison Gardner	Waitrose Ltd	**Chris Walker**	United Biscuits
Brandon Headlee	ConAgra Foods	**Chris Ward**	Booker Ltd
Yvonne van Heck	ISA Cert	**Sarah Whiting**	ASDA Stores Ltd
Sarah Hesketh	The Co-operative Group	**Jared Winder**	ASDA Stores Ltd
Juliette Jahaj	Sainsbury's Supermarkets Ltd		

We would also like to thank the following sites and Certification Bodies that kindly participated in trial audits to test the Standard:

Cavaghan and Gray – Carlisle

Fyffes Group Limited – Wakefield Ripening Centre

Pinnacle Foods

Northern Foods

SAI Global

Knight International Inspectorate

The British Retail Consortium is also pleased to acknowledge the helpful contributions provided by individuals and organisations from across the globe:

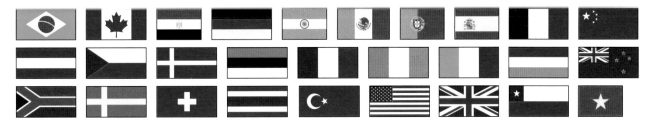

AS Santa Maria/Saue Production OÜ

ASDA Stores Ltd

Bakkavor Ltd

Blue Moon Ltd

British Frozen Food Federation

British Meat Processors Association

Campden BRI

Certification Body Co-operation Group:
Australia and New Zealand

Certification Body Co-operation Group: France

Certification Body Co-operation Group:
German Speaking

Certification Body Co-operation Group: Netherlands

Certification Body Co-operation Group:
North America

Certification Body Co-operation Group:
Spain and Portugal

Certification Body Co-operation Group: Sweden

Certification Body Co-operation Group: UK

Chilled Food Association

Clemence Technical Services

COFRAC

Coles

Compsey Creamery

Conserve Italia

Coppenrath & Wiese GmbH & Co

Cranswick plc

CSM Bakery Products

DAUCY-COMPAGNIE GENERALE DE CONSERVES

Del Monte Foods

Food and Drink Federation

Fountain Frozen Ltd

Fourayes Farm Ltd

Freiberger Group

Fresh Pak Chilled Foods

Fresh Produce Consortium

GEHLKOPF Conseil Eurl

Haasen Consultancy BV

Iceland Foods Ltd

Iverk Produce Ltd

J Foster Consulting

Moulton Bulb Co. Ltd (British Onions Chairman)

Mycotoxin Laboratory (UK) Ltd

North American TAC

Odom's Tennessee Pride

Pestproof Ltd

Precon Food Management

Produce World

Sainsbury's Supermarket Ltd

Santa Maria AB

Seafood Products Association

Shoda Sauces Europe Company Limited

Soleco UK Ltd

Sonneveld Group B.V.

The Cooperative Group

The First Milk Cheese Company

The Wine and Spirit Trade Association

TIPIAK TRAITEUR PATISSIER

Tyson Foods, Inc.

UWIC

VeilleAlim.eu

Waitrose Ltd

Water Brands Group

Weetabix Ltd

WM Morrison Supermarkets PLC